COUNTRYMAN:

A Summary of Belief

Other Books by Hal Borland

Hal Borland

COUNTRYMAN:
A SUMMARY OF BELIEF

J. B. LIPPINCOTT COMPANY
Philadelphia and New York

PRINTED IN THE UNITED STATES OF AMERICA

Library of Congress Catalog Card Number: 65-13694

To Barbara—"There was a star danced . . ."

Foreword

It is in the nature of man to try to draw a tally line somewhere and say, "This much I know. These things I believe." But summaries are elusive things because change is the one constant in this world. Today's truth may be only another myth by tomorrow, and a belief stated now is sure to bristle with questions before the ink is dry. Being aware of change, therefore, I undertook a year ago to set down what seemed to be valid observations of man's estate and his relationship to his environment, not as dicta or ultimate statements but as a summary of belief at this point. I began it in May, the month of my birth, and now I find that it reflects a year of my growing older and, perhaps, wiser; at least, of coming full circle with myself. This book is the result.

There is an old saying that there is nothing new except what has been forgotten. Perhaps I have been trying to restate things known and forgotten many times by other countrymen. If they seem new, I suspect that most of them are new only in that sense. But I happen to believe that the old and the forgotten need restatement from time to time, if only as reminders.

Memories, after all, are the roots of understanding. Without a yesterday, today is meaningless.

Being a personal statement, this book inevitably deals with personal beliefs. For example, I believe that most of man's thorny problems are created, not by this world in which he lives, but by man himself: his ignorance, his stubbornness, his arrogance, his plain human cussedness. I am not convinced of either human perfectibility or inherent damnation; nor do I believe that man is the final and perfect flower of evolution or that the world and the universe exist only for man's pleasure and possession. Biologically speaking, many other forms of life are far more efficient and enduring than man has yet proved himself to be. But man does seem unique in his capacity to dream, to reason, to plan, to enjoy and, unhappily, to punish and destroy. And, as I am proving at this moment, to communicate.

Such beliefs lead to questions to which no one knows all the answers. Perhaps there are no answers, but if there are I am sure they will not be read from a column of statistics or flashed out by an electronic computer. They will be reasoned and deliberated, and they will take into account things a man learns only by being aware of the universe, sensing the earth beneath his feet, participating in the seasons, acknowledging his own limitations, and trying to understand his relationship to the infinitude of life around him.

As a result of a commitment in which I had no part, the commitment of life itself, I have been for years watching, sensing, participating, and trying to understand, and I still find no ultimate answers. But perhaps I have achieved some awareness of the scope of the questions. I doubt that anyone can live with sunrise and moonset, bud and falling leaf, flow of live water and stubborn stand of the hills, and avoid such awareness. This book is a report on that commitment, an account of what has been happening inside and around one countryman during one brief span of this mysterious voyage through time and space.

H. B.
Salisbury, Conn.
1964

Contents

COUNTRYMAN:

A Summary of Belief

1

THE HILLS STILL STAND

March and April passed and I admit that I drew a cautious sigh of relief when May Day arrived. The astrologers were wrong. The planets they were watching converged, but as far as I can make out the hills still stand. Those that I can see from here, anyway; and the disaster-hunters have not yet sent back any travelogues of the Himalayas tottering. It looks as though Spring, and maybe even Summer, is safe for another year, whatever happens to man.

I don't think of myself as a jittery man, and those who seek and find portents in the stars and planets seldom worry me. But when they said how many astral bodies were lining up for some dire purpose a few weeks back I began to wonder. Outer space, as we call it, is a big place, but there seem to be a good many things wandering around out there besides the assortment of hardware that man has flung into orbit; and I am not sure that anyone knows what would happen if half a dozen of them headed our way at once.

Then we had an unseasonably hot spell during what were supposed to be the crucial few days, and a man who says he is privy to important matters phoned me and said, "Feel that heat? This is It!" I asked what was It, and he exulted, "The Big Bonfire!" As nearly as I could make out, somebody, or Some Thing, on Mars or perhaps Saturn or Jupiter, had pressed the button.

My friend hung up and I went outdoors, prepared to make my peace with the universe. But things were little different from what they had been twenty-four hours earlier and I put off my peace-making. My quarrel is with mankind anyway, not with universalities. And that night the warm spell ended.

I haven't heard from my omniscient friend since. Maybe he used the wrong key to break the code. Up to now, at least, the human predicament has not been resolved in one quick flash, from outer space or anywhere else.

Meanwhile, the birds came back and the buds opened and Spring got down to business pretty much as usual. Up here in the hills we got the fences mended and the plowing done and the oats in, and pretty soon we will be planting corn. Next week, in fact. Some of the daily crises will just have to wait till we get caught up with the farm work. We won't be much help until that brief spell between corn planting and haying, which starts about the first of June.

I am speaking for a diminishing minority, of course—the countrymen. The Census Bureau lists about 30 per cent of the population as rural, but that includes residents in towns and villages of up to 2,500 population; only about 8 per cent of us actually live on farms, and the trend is still away from the land, they say. When I write periodic reports from my own rural valley, I often feel like a foreign correspondent. I may yet need a passport to visit the city. But even here in the hills we are, thanks to modern communication, constantly within earshot of the world's worries and lamentations as well as its occasional shouts of triumph.

Out in the back pasture the other morning I watched a woodchuck cleaning out his den. I saw that 'chuck the day he emerged from hibernation a month ago. He had slept through more than six months of assorted dangers, including the cold, white fallout that I call snow, and he emerged from his fallout shelter interested in only two things—a mate and something to eat. He found both, of course, and satisfied his basic hungers, and now he was cleaning out the burrow under an old stone wall and preparing for another Summer. As I watched him and remembered his emergence in early April, for a few minutes I had the uneasy feeling that I was witness to a preview of a drama based on the forecasts of seers who foretell the future by examining the entrails of the atom. Then I noticed that this particular woodchuck, at least, did not have anything that looked like a Geiger counter. He was just a woodchuck doing what woodchucks always do and, as far as I could see, with no notion of exterminating his whole race.

I stood there watching that woodchuck, and I heard the red-winged blackbirds down along the river, and I saw the robins and the meadow larks searching for worms and insects in the meadow grass. I saw the bright, new leaves on the birches beyond the pasture. The compulsion of May was working away, down at the root of things, one of the oldest and most insistent forces I know, the force that makes seeds sprout and eggs hatch and flowers bloom.

I wondered if this statistical drift away from the land, from the weather and the seasons and all their inescapable evidence, might in some way be responsible for such reports as the one I puzzled over for several cold, rainy March days. It was the statement by certain men of science who believe that human beings have a kind of compulsion toward race suicide. As I read and interpreted their words, man works his way slowly up from cave culture toward civilization just so he can eventually kick the props out from under the whole thing. Then somebody, or something, has to start all over again. If by chance one man and one woman are left after the roof falls in, it is up to them to start the long climb toward disaster again. But if everybody goes, then it will be up to the insects, or the salamanders maybe, or some other form of slowly evolving life.

A few days after I wrestled with that report I found another one that seemed to tie in. Somebody had been testing porpoises, had found them to be intelligent, and had even worked out a phonetic alphabet for the porpoise language. And the thought occurred that somebody had picked the porpoise to inherit the deadly mantle of civilization. With that phonetic alphabet we could hail an old bull porpoise, when the time comes, and say, "So long, Buster. Here goes nothing. Now *you're* it." Maybe porpoises would be better than woodchucks, at that. Woodchucks know how to manage underground, but porpoises, I understand, have a sense of humor.

Somehow, out there in the back pasture the other morning, with May all around me, I couldn't believe a word of it. Maybe the season was at work in my bloodstream and my glands, but it did seem to me that if we are ingenious enough to learn to talk to a porpoise, surely we could find a way to make ourselves understood to each other, no matter whether the language is English, Russian, Chinese, or Bantu. And if civilization must lead to a suicidal imperative, then we should be able to find some means of not being so damned civilized.

On the way back to the house I picked a few wild violets to give to my wife, who is sentimental about such things. Some men give their women diamonds and mink stoles, and down in Texas they give them monogrammed airplanes. Up here in the hills we aren't that civilized.

I picked the violets, and on my way back to the kitchen door I passed the garden, freshly plowed and mellow, warm and fragrant with Spring. The peas are in and up, and so is the first lettuce and the first row of beans, though they still look rather spindly. I decided that if the weather holds we should risk planting the first sweet corn next week. Then I remembered my grandmother and her garden. Peas and beans and corn, she said, should always be planted in a growing moon, between the first quarter and the full. All crops that grow above the ground, she insisted, do best under a growing moon. But radishes, beets, carrots, potatoes, all underground crops, had to be planted when the moon was "in the decline," between the full moon and the last quarter.

I couldn't remember offhand which phase the moon was in when we planted those peas and early beans. I would have to look it up. But I did know that the moon is now in its first quarter. I wouldn't say I am superstitious, and we have never planted a garden by the moon. But when the Space Agency in Washington thinks the moon is so important that we should spend I don't remember how many billion dollars to send a man there and stake out a claim, who am I to laugh it off? Grandma was not much of a scientist, but she must have been on the right track.

We shall get the early corn in the ground tomorrow, while the moon is right. With that much of an investment in the moon, I wonder if it wouldn't be a good idea to have the Peace Corps, or somebody, pass the word around in the Congo and Vietnam and other hungry places that corn should be planted in a waxing moon. Rice, too, I should think, since rice also grows above the ground.

I came in and gave the violets to my wife, and she put them

in a tiny vase and set them on the kitchen window sill. They were beautiful, in a quiet way; but here in the house they made me think of the lone first violet I found and picked for her the first week in April. That one small blossom held the whole sweet promise of Spring and we exclaimed over it, treasured it. Now we have plenty of violets, if we look for them, and the pasture margins are rich with a variety of wild flowers. Perversely human, we cherish the rare and take the abundant for granted. The first flower is an event, whether it is a daffodil you buy at a florist shop, a hyacinth you grow in a greenhouse, or a violet you find blooming beside the brook. The newness was gone. These violets were just violets now.

That afternoon we went down to the bog to see if the yellow lady's slippers were in bloom. They were barely in sight a month ago when we went there to get a mess of marsh marigolds at the proper stage for Spring greens. Now the lady's slippers were just opening bud. We found three in blossom and had that thrill of discovery we always get at seeing them. And left them alone, as they should be left, safe from hot, acquisitive human hands, so that they will persist and bloom again next year, and next. Unless someone drains the bog, of course.

Having found the lady's slippers, we retreated to firm, dry land and sat on the grass to look and listen and feel the special air of any natural swampy place.

The meadow that sloped down to the bog had patches of bluets blooming, *Houstonia caerulea,* which some call "quaker-ladies" and some call "innocence." They were like little patches of fog in the grass, for they grew close to each other and bloomed profusely. The tiny four-petaled flowers were so white, so lightly touched with any shade of blue, that I wondered why any one ever called them "bluets." And at the wet margin of the swamp the long-stemmed violets made a mass of velvety purple, one of the richest colors early May has to offer. But it was the bog itself that was dominant.

Redwings challenged us at first, for we were strangers, aliens. They circled and scolded and flashed their crimson epaulettes, and they perched on last year's cattails, swaying precariously. The old cattails were fluffed into smoky-looking tufts, ragged out by wind and Winter and perhaps by the early nest builders too. Somewhere down among them the female blackbirds, sparrowy in their inconspicuous plumage, were already nesting. At the base of each cattail stalk rose the bright green of new growth, blades that had begun to make the bog a miniature jungle. Among them was the darker green of blue flag, the wild iris, which will color the swampland in another month with its big blossoms. At this stage the blades of iris and cattails look much alike except that the cattails are somewhat narrower and a lighter, yellower green. And among them were the still narrower blades of one of the bur reeds, probably *symplex,* whose blades look almost like rank grass.

On and around the tussocks that stood above the water were marsh marigolds, nearly all of them in bloom. Some were up to their ears in water, the leaves seeming to float and the blossoms only a little higher. They are cousins of the meadow buttercups and the Latin name, *Caltha palustris,* means "marsh cup." Botanically, they are also cousins of the wild columbine; but that is one of those things I have to take on faith. I don't really believe it, though I know it is true—how can cousins have such totally different flowers?

On the tussocks themselves were great masses of skunk cabbage leaves, big as elephant ears, gaudy, extravagant, and primitive. And among them I could see others of the arum family, a few jack-in-the-pulpits with their dark-striped green spathes, a number of light green, plantain-like leaves of sweet flag, and an occasional dart-shaped leaf of the arrow arum.

On the far margin of the little bog were two tall elms still trembling on the verge of full leaf, still lacy with tufts of young seeds. Beneath them were clumps of willow brush where the inch-long leaves had already begun to hide the finished male catkins that were tiny pussy willows six weeks ago. And alder brush was tufting out in leaf, still hung with little cone-like seed cases from last year. From somewhere nearby a hyla shrilled and I thought he was the last, late member of the Spring peeper chorus that was so loud two weeks before. Then from down at the other end of the bog came an answer in a hyla voice so high and shrill it sounded like falsetto. But there was no chorus, just those two tardy peepers trilling at each other from time to time.

The bog water was a kind of pewter gray, though it glinted here and there, reflecting the afternoon sunlight when a red-wing flew from a cattail stem and launched a ripple from its base. But it had a green tint, too, bright and lively. Duckweed, finer than the finest confetti, had already put out its tiny leaves and floated on that pewter surface.

There was a dark movement back among the cattails. As we watched, a big brown muskrat swam into the open, the V of ripples from his nose like long, silvery whiskers. He swam toward the bank where we sat, and suddenly he saw us and dived with a plop and left only a swirling of the dark water where he had been.

We sat there for half an hour, and I had the feeling I always get in the presence of a bog. It is as though I stood on the brink of ancient days when warm seas washed the first land and aquatic life was making its first venture away from the mother element, water. I am a witness to primal beginnings, a participant somehow in elemental change. All things seem possible, there on the bank where the teeming bog waters meet the waiting land. The very smell of a bog is fecund and fertile of mysterious and fundamental life evolving. Toward my kind of creature? Perhaps, but not necessarily. Except in my most egocentric moments I hesitate to believe that evolution inevitably is pointed toward man as its ultimate goal. Evolution is change, and man may be a biological accident; it is too soon to know, for man seems to have been here only a million years or so, whereas life probably has been evolving at least a thousand times that long.

Sometimes, particularly toward dusk of a Summer evening, I get the feeling that if I were to stay there by the margin of those bog waters for just another five minutes I might see a thirty-foot stegosaurus, complete with armor-plate scales, come wading out from among the reeds and cattails, trailing a million centuries behind him. I have never waited those extra five minutes, perhaps because I am more cowardly than curious. Someday before I die I hope to muster the courage.

We didn't wait that afternoon. But as we left the bog and started home I wondered why our reclamationists persist in draining the wetlands of this earth. Aside from all the economic reasons for not draining them, which are too many to discuss here, we need bogs and swamplands to remind us of beginnings. Especially now, when we are so obsessed with endings. If we had a lick of sense we would send a delegation of thoughtful observers to the swamps, just to look and listen and think, and then come back and tell us what they learned. From time to time some naturalist makes his report on a particular bogland, but it seldom gets much circulation beyond the circle of naturalists who already know most of the scientific facts about swamps. What I have in mind would have fewer

Latin names and more of a sense of destiny. I suspect that far more is to be learned from the swamps than from the stars, or even from the moon.

I wouldn't attempt such a report, but if I did I would remember that life began in the swamps and that is where the first little ratlike mammals took up the challenge and began the long climb toward supremacy over the giant lizards. I might even start by naming one of those primitive little mammals George and calling the top-dog dinosaur a dragon. The story from there could be quite exciting, if one didn't get involved in suicidal imperatives.

History—and I am thinking in considerably larger terms than human history; I am reaching for the history of life—seems to have been always a matter of challenge, challenge accepted or rejected. And the insistent, decisive challenges probably have always been those of weather and environment. Weather has forced life forms to some means of adaptation, and environment has persistently and continually sorted and chosen those life forms which would persist. There has been no successful appeal from those two challenges and their demands.

Now if we narrow our sense of history to the brief span of human life, we find that those same two challenges have always been decisive—the weather and the land. Few if any civilizations of consequence have evolved except in the temperate zones with their alternating seasons of warmth and cold. Even the Aztec and Inca cultures here in America, though in the tropics, flowered in mountain areas where altitude created the equivalent of temperate-zone climate, the Aztecs in 7,500-foot Mexico City, the Incas in 11,000-foot

Cuzco. And every civilization of which we have record has been dependent on the land, for food, for water, for raw materials, even for strengthening infusions of sturdy, land-nurtured peasant blood.

Without challenge, man is essentially a lazy lout. The long story of civilizations is a chronicle of challenges met, mastered, and followed by periods of ease. Ease begot sloth, sloth begot weakness, and new tribes, new nations rose to dominance. When man became a lazy lout again, as he did repeatedly, he lost not only his ease but his whole inheritance to other men still eager to accept the challenge.

On the way back from the bog we took the shortcut through the woods and over the hill. From the hilltop we could look out across the valley and see half a dozen small farms with their pasturelands lush and green with May. Two farmers were out with tractors plowing old fields that will be planted with corn in another week or two. I could almost smell the fresh-turned soil, sweeter than the swamp muck by far, but also rich with the odors of fertility and potent beginnings. The land, the challenge of the land.

I am reluctant to equate sweat and blisters with virtue, but I did remember the old aphorism that the devil finds work for idle hands. I haven't heard those words in a long time. Maybe they were quietly ruled unconstitutional, since we now have government agencies to find recreational occupation for idle hands and other agencies to help create more leisure, more idleness. But as I looked at those fields in this long-settled corner of the New England hills, I thought of the slow plod of oxen and the sweaty backs of plowmen, men too busy making a living from the land to wonder or worry long about the civilization they were building. They seldom called it civilization, for that matter. They called it a way of life, and they hoped for a better tomorrow.

Looking across the valley at this land alive with May and Spring, I wondered what sustained those pioneering men and women, what harvest they achieved beyond their daily bread. Then I remembered the day-end thoughts the literate among them set down in letters and diaries, old-fashioned notions about the virtue of work and the satisfaction of accomplishment. Yes, and the belief that everything, including leisure and peace and freedom, had its price. The offhand words of one old countryman came back to me. "My grandfather used to say to me," he told me, "that the land won't ever love you, but it won't hate you, either. Nature, he always said, is too busy with creation to have time for hate."

And I thought that was one reason the hills still stand, despite the convergence of the planets and all the other direful things. Maybe that explains why there is an insistent human urge to get out and see a tree, a brook, a meadow, and look and listen, and let the land heal the hurts and bruises of civilization. A civilization that too often forgets those basic challenges, the land and the weather, and turns instead to the challenge of man to man.

2

SUMMER AND THE SENSE
OF TIME

The first cutting of hay is in and under cover, the corn is almost knee-high, the solstice is just ahead, and Summer is almost upon us. Another year is about to pass its midpoint and the countryman takes comfort in the fact that there are four seasons in every year, four spans of time that are not dependent on machines that go tick-tick-tick. Despite the urgencies of man's own follies, there is a kind of time that doesn't have to be measured in minutes, seconds, and microseconds. For those who would look for it, June provides the corrective, the essential pause that should restore perspective.

It is heresy, of course, for any countryman to admit that there is any season of the year when he isn't driven by the clock. But the fact is that most of us living on the land could throw away both clocks and calendars and still get along. The sun rises and sets on schedule, Summer comes when the urgencies of Spring begin to abate, and Autumn always follows Summer. Here in my valley we don't have to look at the calendar to know when it is time to plant corn, or mow hay, or harvest oats, or dig potatoes. If it is important to know the month, June is the time when hay is ready to be cut, and potatoes should be dug in September, certainly no later than October. But even those notations on nature's clock are matters of comfort and convenience rather than of compulsion.

For instance, it doesn't matter to the grass whether the farmer cuts it before it goes to seed or not. That is up to the farmer. If he doesn't cut it, the seed ripens and falls and fills in the bare spots with new grass next year. That, after all, is the function of seed, to grow. Man knows that grass makes good hay for his livestock if it is properly cured, and if he heeds the natural clock he gets his hay. But even then it doesn't matter whether he cuts it at ten minutes after eight in the morning or at high noon, just so it is properly cured before he stows it away. The sun tolls off the countdown for hay, as well as for a good many other things, and the sun can be very deliberate in June.

What it amounts to, really, is a choice between freedom and security, and the result usually is a compromise. The farmer is free to cut hay or not, and to cut it when he chooses. But if he would have the security of plenty he must curb that freedom somewhat and obey certain natural restrictions. Otherwise he will find himself scrounging among the roots of the field and the nuts of the woodland to keep from starving to death.

That is the dilemma of freedom in the big, theoretical sense, as we are constantly reminded, whether we take heed or not. And it is also the complication that makes security so elusive, despite the fine theories and the often frantic experiments. Absolute freedom and complete security are not really compatible, as a good many of the new nations of this world are discovering so painfully today, and as most of the old ones find it so difficult to admit. Neither man nor nation can make hay, either literally or figuratively, without compromise somewhere.

Standing on the riverbank soon after sunrise this morning, I had, for a few moments, a sense of foreverness that now seems so uncommon. Time stood still for a little while and the day ahead seemed endless. June and Summer were an infinity of time, boundless. Then I thought of the day itself and all its chores and obligations, and the illusion was gone. But for a few moments I had reached back into small boyhood, when time had wholly different dimensions.

When I was eight or nine years old I knew when school closed in early June that it would open again in September, but meanwhile there were countless long days to go fishing, play Pan with dandelion stems, roam the countryside, eat green apples, or just lie in the grass and watch towering cumulus clouds drift lazily past. Life was not complicated by either freedom or security, since I had both in large measure and was not actually aware of either. That birthright of childhood, in my day at least, conferred a special sense of time which really amounted to a kind of timelessness.

This morning, after those few minutes of timelessness on the riverbank, I wondered if that boyhood sense of time was something personal that had vanished with my own past. Then, while out for a walk early this afternoon, I met a small boy on the riverbank, where he was fishing. I said, "Hi," and sat down beside him and waited, watching his bobber. "How are they biting?" I finally asked.

"Not very good today," he said, watching a dragonfly hover. Then he brightened. "Yesterday I caught four, though. I'm going to catch a thousand fish this Summer!"

Being a grownup, I made a mental calculation. At four a

day, his Summer was going to be at least eight months long. "What else are you going to do this Summer?" I asked.

"Oh, lots of things. Eddie and I are building a tree house. And I'm making a rock collection. Did you know there are garnets, real garnets, in the rocks on that hill right up the road? I found seven there last week. I'm going to learn how to polish gems this Summer. And when we go to the shore for Daddy's vacation I'll get more shells for my shell collection."

His bobber jiggled and went under and he caught a fish, a rock bass and not very big, but another fish of that thousand he is going to catch this Summer. I wished him well and walked on up the road, my question about boyhood and time at least partly answered.

Walking up the road, I thought how fortunate that boy was, and what an exceptional life he lives, up here where he can come alone to a riverbank and watch a hovering dragonfly and fish for rock bass and think his own thoughts. By the current canons that prevail in too many places, he would be drafted into some supervised group activity thought up by adults. And I thought of a small boy in San Diego who wrote a letter to the President of the United States. He said that the California canyon where he and his pals used to hunt lizards and watch the sky was being taken over for a housing development and he asked if the President couldn't set aside land where boys like him could play. The President sent the letter along to the Secretary of the Interior for an answer.

The Secretary wrote to this boy, saying in part that "we have a great awareness of the need to be able to hunt lizards and follow ants or maybe just lie in the sun on your back and watch the changing shape of clouds—alone. We are trying to set aside some land where you can play—not in groups with supervision, but just roaming around by yourself and finding out how you relate to the earth and sky. It's a thing you can do only by yourself and it's a very important thing."

It was a good letter, and the ideas were right as rain. Boys— and girls, and grownups as well—desperately need places where they can watch lizards and ants, and chipmunks and dragonflies and frogs and bumblebees. They need places where they can sit on a riverbank or lie in the sun and see the sky without looking for satellites or ICBM's. That is what the conservationists have been talking about for a long, long time.

And that point about doing it alone, not in a group or under supervision, that is one of the most important points of all and one too often ignored. It sometimes seems that in this age of organization we have lost sight of the individual. Every-thing from singing to games, from travel to nature-watching, has become a group activity. The person who wants to do anything alone, even just sit and think, has to fight off the organizers. We have even coined a derogatory term for the person who likes now and then to be alone with the world— we call such a person antisocial, as though he were an enemy of society. We are not content to say that he is nonsocial. In the modern lexicon, *non* means *anti*.

Yet many things in this world, including one's own identity, have to be discovered alone. Maybe that is why so many people are lost and bewildered, intellectually and emotionally —they never get the chance to find themseves. They are for-ever lost in a crowd. From nursery school on, they are told over and over that social adaptation and participation are essential, that social adjustment is the enduring purpose, and that if they persist in going their own way they will be misfits, doomed to failure. Conformity is the end toward which they are constantly urged, conformity to the crowd.

Conformity really isn't the only thing in life. "Just roaming around by yourself and finding out how you relate to the earth and sky" is important too, perhaps the most important thing of all. I wish more small boys' parents understood that, and more teachers. It would even be satisfying if some of those in high places in Washington and the state capitols understood it too, and remembered it when they draw up plans for mass housing and mass recreation and all the other group projects that get so much attention.

This really isn't such a crowded country, as we keep telling ourselves it is, except in certain areas. Too many of our sociologists and social planners fail to stand on a stool and look over the heads of the crowd before they diagnose and prescribe. There are a good many hilltops left, and a good many woodlands, even though the cities and their crawling suburbs extend in all directions. Most of the planning, however, is done by those who see the sprawl and and ignore the space. To them, that small boy in San Diego is not a person but a population unit. They would plan group activities for him, supervise him, adjust him, when what he wants, what he needs, is a chance to be himself. He needs a chance to go out and find a lizard—or fish for rock bass, or watch a dragonfly, or find garnet crystals—all by himself. In so doing, he may find some small part of himself.

That is what we all need, isn't it? Maybe that is what we miss, in this abundant life of organized groups. We have become so obsessed with the new folklore of statistics that we seem to forget the fundamental truths behind them. It is possible that there aren't too many people, though I am sure that is open to debate; and it is more than possible that there aren't enough individuals, enough people who know how they relate to the earth and the sky and even to themselves.

I came on up the road, but before I got home I heard a cicada shrilling, that piercing sound that starts as a buzz, rises to a stridulous shriek, then dies away like an alarm clock running down. That cicada was a late arrival, remnant of the minor hordes we had a few weeks ago. This was a year of the seventeen-year locusts, and for a couple of weeks they dinned in my woodland and gorged on leaves and made the customary threat of devastation that they seldom carry out. Then they vanished, as they always do, and we weren't devastated. Even the few trees they half denuded will put out enough new leaves by the end of this month to tide them over safely.

I didn't stop to listen to this lone cicada-locust today, as I might have in other years. I am rather tired of that stridulated shriek and what it stands for, just as I am tired of the superstitions about those locusts. Because the red veins on their wings make a pattern like a W, some otherwise sensible people say their appearance in unusual numbers portends war. They seem to forget that W also stands for welcome and wisdom and wedding and well-being, as well as a number of other unwarlike things. Besides, like so many omens, this one has two sides to it. Looked at from the other side, those veins form an M, not a W, and M stands for music and moderation and magnanimity and merrymaking and, if one must be crass, even for money.

Besides being dubious prophets, these locusts participate in still another phase of time. They are among the longest lived of all insects, seventeen years in the North, thirteen years in the South. But they spend most of their lives in a larval stage underground, unperturbed by seasons or sex or wind or weather. When they finally emerge they molt and become mature winged insects which have a week or two of adult life that they spend eating, flying awkwardly from tree to tree, mating, and laying eggs. Then they die. The eggs quietly hatch, the new larvae burrow into the ground, and the long, dark cycle starts all over again.

As mature insects, the periodic locusts know time only as a matter of days, even of hours. Listening to the shrill calls of the males to the silent females, I always sense a frantic urgency in them. Hurry, hurry, hurry! Hurry for what? To return to the long, deliberate, insensible larval stage where time isn't even measured in weeks or months, but in years. I hear them every Summer, since a few of them are out of phase, so to speak, and not members of the periodic hordes. And every time I hear them I am reminded of two-legged creatures who also shout, "Hurry, hurry, hurry!" I wonder what we are urging ourselves to hurry toward. Could it be the security of some insensitive larval stage of existence too?

But it is Summer now, most of the locusts have committed their inheritance to the egg and the larva, and the outdoor tempo is back to order. Spring's urgencies are largely past. The great green canopy of chlorophyll is spread and the deliberate process of photosynthesis goes on with no fuss whatever. The early nesting of the birds is completed and the fledglings are on the wing. Trees that were a shimmering glory of white blossoms in May are now hung with little green apples that won't ripen till September. The brooks have relaxed into gurgling passage across the meadow, their spate gone down to the sea. The long, slow swing of the pendulum toward

Autumn will soon begin, deliberate as the drone of a sated bumblebee on a hot afternoon. The world abounds in natural aspects of plenty and tranquillity. And here am I, here is mankind, to participate if we only will.

True, nature has her hungers and her necessities, even in Summer. The red fox stalks my meadow for mouse and rabbit. The kingfisher dives into my river for a piscine meal. The harmless robin struts my lawn with a cocked head and pounces on the unwary angleworm. Big bugs eat little bugs in my garden and all my fields. But all without rancor or passion. Nature commits no crimes. Nature does not deal in morality, which is a concept peculiar to man and, I find, somewhat fluctuant even with him.

I have yet to find evidence that nature has any motive beyond the insistence of life itself. There certainly is neither charity nor malevolence in nature, nor any degree of either punishment or pardon. Rain falls on the just and the unjust alike, and so does hail; and I have never noticed that earthquake or tornado, flood or lightning bolt, chooses among the reverent, the profane, the industrious, and the lazy when it strikes. Despite man's long habit of endowing sun, moon, stars, weather, and other natural elements and forces with anthropomorphic passions and sensibilities, it is my experience that the patterns of nature's behavior are quite unrelated to man's wishes, his needs, or even his prayers.

But because man seems always to have been reluctant to accept the responsibility for his own folly, he long ago conceived a pantheon of gods to take the blame and, on rare occasions, to get the credit and receive his thanks. At one time or another, almost everything from an oak tree to a volcano, from a serpent to the east wind—in addition to all the weather gods—was so endowed and canonized. No one who believes the truth of nature can too much quarrel with this; but the reasonable person must recognize that man did thereby establish an inner contradiction that still persists and on occasion can create a good deal of mischief. In one breath we speak of destiny and imperatives, and in the next breath we boast of our knowledge and our powers of ultimate decision. You can't go on forever passing the buck and at the same time issuing orders.

And that, if I may for a moment lapse into the kind of thinking I have just now deplored, is one reason for Summer. Man needs such a season to help repair his perspective in terms of time, and he needs the annual abundance that persists in spite of his own bungling to make him realize, however dimly, the existence of forces greater than his own will and imagination. A periodic swallow of humility, however bitter it may be going down, never hurt any of us.

So here we are in the midst of June. Sunlight and rain have no price tags, and nobody has ever rationed the number of leaves on a tree. Shakespeare's books in brooks are still uncensored, and neither Congress nor the Supreme Court has repealed the laws of growth. The last time I looked, the moon was right on schedule; it will come to the full one week from tonight whether the sky be clear or cloudy. And I can testify that water still runs downhill, for the Housatonic River, just beyond my dooryard, is at this moment flowing toward Long Island Sound some 100-odd miles to the south and downhill all the way.

Things seem to be pretty well in order, even to small boys who still think that Summer lasts a long, long time if not quite forever. The hay is in, and the hayfields are green with their second growth. The corn will soon be laid by, as we say, cultivated for the last time. The countryman has time to catch his breath, and the city man and his family have time to take a vacation. Even business, the transactions of man to man, can get along shorthanded for a few weeks. Epidermis by the square yard is being exposed to sunburn and mosquitoes. Female mosquitoes; the males don't bite, which is another reason for that discerning French exclamation, *"Vive la différence!"* Fireflies wink their mysterious lights at dusk and long into the warm, starlit night.

June, and Summer, and I am pleased that no Summer does last forever. We need that reminder. Without the fact of Summer, and the awareness that Summer passes, how would we know when Winter comes that no Winter lasts forever either?

3

THE RIPENING OF
INDEPENDENCE

July is the year's high noon, mid-Summer and virtually a season unto itself. Now the ant and the bee and even the awkward beetle put the busy countryman to shame for a sluggard, and the quiet chlorophyll in the green leaf makes man's fissioned atom a puny force by comparison. The change that has come over this earth since April would be incredible if we didn't see it happen every year and know it is as inevitable as sunrise. But miracles lose their wonder when even the laity can predict them, as the shamans learned long ago. One sprouting kernel of corn is an astonishing, marvelous thing; but a cornfield in Iowa is just another crop maturing, another consequence of a farmer cooperating with the soil and the seasons. You might call it another kink in the Gordian knot of the farm surplus problem if you want to spend the rest of the Summer arguing politics and economics. I don't.

As a countryman whose only corn crop is sweet corn for my own table, I always come to July with a special sense of independence. Part of this, I am sure, is because in a few more days we shall be observing the anniversary of the Declaration of Independence. Some of us will, and several million others will be celebrating a long weekend holiday made incalculably grim by the grisly forecasts of the National Safety Council. I shall be staying home, cherishing life, liberty, and the pursuit of happiness in a simple, rural way. But I shall be thinking about the Declaration and the way it came into being.

The timing may have been dictated by other reasons, which I am sure the historians can cite, but any countryman must believe that the season had something to do with it. It was June 7, 1776, when Richard Henry Lee, who called himself a Virginia farmer, laid before the Continental Congress a resolution that the colonies be considered free and independent. Four days later a committee of five was named to draft a resolution to that effect. Of those five men, Thomas Jefferson, Roger Sherman, and John Adams were close enough to the land to call themselves farmers in one degree or another. They knew the land. Jefferson, who was chosen to write the text, was a muddy-boots farmer who knew soil and crops and who even invented a new and better plow.

It was almost mid-June when the committee got down to work. The land that Jefferson knew so well and loved so completely was burgeoning. The days seemed, as they still seem, specially shaped for a man to till and prepare the harvest that will ensure his safety and independence. Any June is full of promise, the growing strength of July's abundance. The first hay has been cut and cured. Pastures are lush. Corn is shooting up and oats are beginning to head. By the end of June any provident Virginia farmer has friers ready for the pan, new potatoes ready for the pot, and fresh garden peas on the table. By July the land itself challenges a man to stand up and proclaim his manhood. The materials for his independence are all around him.

So Thomas Jefferson, farmer, a man still in his thirty-fourth
year, sat in a stuffy Philadelphia room, hungry for his acres
while the solstice passed, and drafted the document which
begins, "When, in the course of human events," and closes,
"with a firm reliance on the protection of Divine Providence,
we mutually pledge our Lives, our Fortunes and our Sacred
Honor." Revised and completed, the Declaration was finally
passed and approved by the Continental Congress on July 4.
Jefferson, by the way, bought a thermometer that day and
noted that the Philadelphia temperature at 9 P.M. was 73.5
degrees. The Declaration was printed in the Philadelphia
newspapers on July 6 and first read in public on July 8. That
day Jefferson bought a barometer to take with the thermometer back to Monticello and make systematic observations of
the weather. He probably hungered for garden lettuce and
fresh cucumbers, too, since his cucumbers usually came to
table, as he put it, by July 8.

I suppose the Declaration of Independence could have been
written in December or January, but I am sure it would have
been a somewhat different document even if Jefferson had
written it. In Winter a man hugs the fire, thinks of comfort
and security, and wonders if his supply of meat and hay will
last out the season. By the time June is merging with July, his
world is as big as all outdoors and a man asks only uninter-
rupted time for his harvest.

As it stands—and has stood, a beacon for freedom-hungry
people, for close to 190 years—the Declaration cuts through to
fundamental matters, forthright as the season itself. In effect,
it asks only that the big problems be solved so that a man can
take care of the little ones for himself. It isn't a demand for
three meals a day and a roof overhead; it is a plea for a man's
right to provide such things for himself and be free and secure
in them. I suspect that Jefferson knew that details of ideology

were less important than a man's right to cut his hay, tend his corn, harvest his oats, butcher his hog, and be beholden to no one. Ideologies are essentially matters for indoor theorizing, but freedom and independence walk the fields and stand on the hilltops.

A small matter of independence came up here in my area a few weeks ago that may demonstrate this point in a minor way. We were still doing the late Spring chores, mending fence, cutting brush along the pasture margins, plowing corn land. We were doing the outdoor jobs that enable a man to see the height of the hills and the breadth of the horizon, feel the earth underfoot, and sense the turn of the seasons. No longer house-bound, we may have been a bit cantankerous in our feeling of independence, maybe even old-fashioned.

Anyway, a communication came from Washington saying there was money available for public works and we should find some way to use it locally. We were urged to suggest a public project, apply for government money, and get started at once. It so happened that there was a public project in our local plans. Our town hall needed repairs and renovation. Washington said that would fit right into the program and we were told to submit plans, apply for the money, and get going.

The selectmen called a town meeting. We still have the venerable town-meeting form of government and all such proposals must be discussed in public and be decided by the vote of those at the meeting. It wasn't a particularly big meeting, but from the start it was an outspoken one. Why was this money available? Well, it seems we are in a distressed area. How come? We aren't in distress! That isn't the point. We are in a distressed *area*. It's a matter of statistics. Down in Washington they chart the country by areas geographically, gather statistics on employment, lump them by areas, and classify the areas as distressed or not distressed. Thirty miles from here is a manufacturing town where a couple of factories have laid off quite a few workers. Geographically we are in that town's area, and when unemployment there reaches a certain point, the whole area, including us, is rated as distressed. That makes us eligible for this money.

We listened to the explanation, and one man said sharply, "We don't need it. We can pay our own way."

Another man said, "The money's there, already appropriated. Somebody's going to spend it. Why shouldn't we?"

That just seemed to set things off.

"It doesn't make sense, asking for money just because it's there."

"We can refuse to take it, can't we?"

"It's government money, and they want to hand it out."

"It's *our* money. Somebody paid it, in taxes. I say turn it down!"

It turned into an indignation meeting, and when the vote was finally taken, only two voters wanted to accept the government money. The proposal was turned down, overwhelmingly. Then the meeting voted to go ahead with the repairs and renovation and pay for it, every cent, with our own local taxes.

It was a gesture, really, and some people still say it was the work of a group of die-hards. Maybe it was, in a sense, but that calls for a definition of what it is that dies so hard here in these old hills. I shan't try to give a full definition, but I must point to some of the things still cherished here. One is pride in self. Another is independence and self-sufficiency. Still another is integrity—we have to live with ourselves and we still have moral and financial conscience. I suppose it boils down to a belief in the old virtues, and one of those virtues goes away back. It consists in paying your own way as a part of the price of freedom.

Nobody at the meeting really objected to spending money when it is needed. Without argument and unanimously the same meeting approved a request for $2,500 for a new, fire-proof door for the vital records vault and another for $4,000 to cover a deficit in the snow-removal budget for last Winter. What was objected to was needless spending of public money and the bureaucratic habit of urging funds on an area that didn't need help. We just don't believe in that kind of thing.

That, as I say, happened a few weeks back, when we hadn't yet planted corn, when Summer was just a promise. If the same proposal were to come up in July, I doubt that there would be even those two dissenting votes. In July, with Summer all around us, we are even more cantankerously independent than we are in April or May.

I sometimes wonder if this sense of independence isn't one of the basic differences, really, between man as a species and most of the other forms of animal life. I am thinking particularly of those creatures which, like man, have a highly organized system of interdependent life. The bees, the ants, and the wasps, for example.

Such social insects fascinate me, in part because they are so successful as biological species—bees and ants are believed to have been in existence in substantially their present form for at least 100 million years—and in part because they seem to have solved, long ago, many of the social problems that still baffle mankind. Theoretically at least we should be able to learn a great deal from them. But the more I learn about them, the less sure I am that they followed the right road of evolution and man followed the wrong one.

I, being a man, am a biased witness, of course. But when I try to summarize the advantages that should follow closely organized social life for any species, I arrive at several grave questions if I try to apply them to the ants, for example.

Group life should, in theory, provide common strength that vastly exceeds that of the individual. There should be far greater efficiency of achievement and there should be, as a result, more permanent results. Thus far, of course, the ants qualify perfectly. One ant is inconsequential, but a whole colony of ants can be overwhelming. The individual ant can accomplish very little, but a colony of ants can dig a vast network of tunnels and build an ant-hill relatively many times larger than the biggest of the Egyptian pyramids. Further, their type of life with a sharp division of labor should produce specialized skills that combine to create marked success for the colony. This, too, is true of the ants. Within the necessities for survival as a species, they are phenomenally successful. And among them are skilled warriors, builders, food gatherers, nurse maids, even farmers who plant fungus, tend it, and harvest and store it in the colony's pantries.

Then I come to other advantages that should arise from such group life, and the judgment shifts. With a stable, self-sufficient form of life there should be some growth of intelligence. But research indicates that at least 95 per cent of an ant's actions are purely instinctive, perhaps 4 per cent are a result of habit, and a possible 1 per cent can be credited to intelligence.

With the society secure and stable, there should be at least a tentative impulse toward improvement, toward changes that the individual in an insecure society could never risk. Yet so far as we know there have been no essential changes in the life and purposes of ant colonies in millions of years. At the very least, in such a society one might expect the eventual appearance of self-subordination and concern for others, the quality we speak of as compassion. Self-subordination is characteristic of the ants, but compassion is, as far as we can discover, totally lacking. The individual counts for nothing and is completely expendable.

I have been thinking particularly of these matters because of what happened in my boat the other day. It is a small boat from which we fish in the river that flows past our dooryard and I keep it moored to a small dock at the riverbank. We hadn't been out on the river in three weeks, partly because we were busy in the vegetable garden and partly because two heavy rains had muddied the water to a point where it was useless to try to fish. Then the water began to clear and we took the afternoon off. I dug a can of worms, rolled back the boat cover, gassed up the outboard motor, and we set out. We weren't fifty yards from the dock when my wife, the tidy one in this family, picked up a rag that I had left in the bottom of the boat the last time we used it. She picked up the rag and exclaimed, "Ants! Look at the ants!"

There under the rag was a colony of black ants, an earth-dwelling species common along the wooded riverbank. Suddenly uncovered when the rag was removed, they swarmed over the whole central part of the boat in excited ant fashion. I cut off the motor, let the boat drift, and we began sweeping them up with a sponge and tossing them overboard. We got about half of them out of the boat and in so doing scattered half a cupful of pupae, the white, rice-shaped so-called ant eggs. This ant colony had moved into the boat and settled. Whether they had hatched the pupae in the boat or not, I do not know. They may have brought them from an earth nest on shore. They must have boarded the boat by coming down one of the mooring lines.

The ants had scattered at our first attack. Now they came scurrying back, intent on saving those white pupae. An ant would dash in, grasp a pupa almost as big as itself, lift it, and stagger off, looking for a new hiding place. So we concentrated on the big, fat pupae and got the ants as they returned. But quite a few got away from us and lugged their awkward burdens up into the decked-in bow of the boat, hid them there and came back for more. They were assembling a nursery up there, so I had to get down on hands and knees and continue the merciless job of extermination in those cramped quarters.

Finally we had the boat reasonably ant-free, but even after I started the motor again and we went up the river and anchored in a cove and put out our lines, stray ants would come out of hiding, find a pupa in a crack and try to carry it to dark safety. We marveled at their persistence but didn't quite muster the compassion to let them have their way. They were intruders and had to be dispossessed.

But in all this ruthless activity, not one ant bit either of us, though I know that they are of a species that can bite hard and leave a tiny wound that will burn half an hour with formic acid. These ants had only one purpose, to perpetuate the race. They weren't even attacking those who were destroying the colony, us. Those that ran away after that first attack didn't even try to save themselves. They came back to save those pupae. That was their instinct, the reason for which they were hatched. I noticed that even a few smaller ants among them, undoubtedly slaves of another, captive species, tried to save those pupae. Too small to carry a pupa by themselves, they teamed up, two working together. They, too, had the same instinct. Slaves though they were, they didn't try to escape or save their own lives. That isn't within the narrow range of an ant's instinct. If self-preservation or any sense of individual identity ever was a minute part of the ant's instinct or impulse, it was bred out over the ages.

And that led to the thought that the ant colony is essentially a collection of individual cells which do their job without the guidance of a real brain. They are a kind of living machine whose sole purpose is to maintain itself, keep running as it has run for 100 million years or more. In that sense, the ant colony is a complete success, though at the expense of the individual. The living machine, the ant colony, has complexity, but it is the complexity of numbers, not of ideas or even of purposes.

And that is the essential difference between a community of ants and a community of human beings. Ants have been doing the same things in precisely the same way since the Tertiary period. Man, probably no more than a million years old as a distinct species, has constantly changed himself individually as well as his kind collectively. And somewhere along the way the human brain evolved, an infinitely complex organ with the power of thought and memory and reason; and the feeling of sympathy we call compassion was developed. Apparently the ants sacrificed that phase of evolution, or whatever it was, somewhere in the remote past, in the interest of the colony, the species.

If it were possible to imagine such a thing as a town meeting of ants such as we held a few weeks ago, there would have been no discussion and nothing like a dissenting vote. There are no decisions in an ant colony because there are no questions. The individual follows instinct. It knows nothing but instinct. It has but one purpose, to perpetuate the colony as colonies have been perpetuated for eons. Freedom has no meaning to an ant.

Being a man, not an ant, I am aware of July as a kind of summary of independence. It is also, in a way, a summary of the year's first half, of that small span of time between the Winter solstice and the Summer solstice. By now the season's trend is clear, whether Spring was early or late, whether May was wet or dry. By now a countryman can gauge his prospects and, if he is of a philosophical turn of mind, weigh his own wisdom and evaluate the validity of his own purposes. Back in April we were glad to see the end of Winter. By mid-October we will welcome hard frost and the end of the growing season. But right now, in July, we exult in Summer, admitting that it is the power and the glory of the earth itself.

A man can live with Summer. He doesn't have to wall and shield himself from it. He can even feel that he is a partner in its achievements, albeit a definitely junior partner. If he gets too arrogant, a July thunderstorm claps his ears or a tornado makes him think twice about the degree of his omnipotence. Summer supplies its own correctives. But if a man is willing to live with it, not try to dictate to it, he makes out surprisingly well. The hours are long and sweat comes' easily; but it always has been difficult to build anything enduring, including freedom and security, without a good deal of hard work, and nobody has yet invented a better lubricant for the gears of human achievement than sweat.

The season actually begins to lean toward Autumn by July, though we are always reluctant to admit it. Once we have passed the solstice we are on the long incline that leads to October and the falling leaf. Daylight begins to shorten. The sun, as we say, is already edging southward once more. Fledglings are on the wing. Bird song has lost its earlier exultancy. Brooks languish in mid-Summer slack and rivers are tepid and lazy. Algae will soon begin to scum the muddy ponds, and then will come the dog days, sluggish with August.

The meadow margins are still white with daisies, but the orange splashes of black-eyed Susans begin to appear, vivid as a van Gogh brush stroke. Queen Anne's lace is like a froth at the country roadside. Milkweed comes to bloom with a tuberose scent for the evening air. The wood thrush still sings its simple contralto song in the twilight, the whippoorwill is loud and insistent in the late dusk, and fireflies freckle the night. But the jubilance of June has settled into the stridulated insistence of the hot-weather insects. July possesses the land.

If ever I realize how completely I am a squatter here, a tenant whose paper deed has no validity except among men, it is in July. Then I know that the earth really belongs to no man, that I or anyone else can live in relative comfort here if I work at it, but in the end I belong to the earth, not the other way round. And the earth has no concern with my human problems, none whatever. I am just another fleck of life in an environment that teems with life. I am outnumbered on every hand. But because I am a man, not an ant, a sentient creature endowed with the capacity for thought and blessed with dreams, I can persist and even have my own small importance for a brief span of time as an individual. If I am wise, I can even maintain a degree of freedom not only among my own kind but upon the earth.

And that is where the dreams come in. What is a dream but an exaltation, a reaching beyond the limits of everyday reality? Without the dream, what is there? There is insect drone, frog croak, starlight, the rhythmic wash of the tides, the sigh of the wind in the trees. But with the dream there is humanity and, in flashes now and then, something we call understanding.

July, mid-Summer, is hospitable to the dream. In a sense, July is January's dream of perfection. Perhaps that is why Thomas Jefferson mustered the words he did with Summer ripening in the country air and his whole being aware of it. To a countryman standing now in the richness of another July, that is explanation enough. The hopes, the dreams, of men who knew Summer on the land came to a proper ripeness in those words.

4

DOG DAYS AND LITTLE GREEN APPLES

The dog days are upon us and I have just had a visit from an apple man. I am surrounded, it seems, by myths and superstitions, including the notion that God made little green apples just for man to hybridize and harvest for the market. Thinking about these matters, I have been hobnobbing with ancient stargazers, amateur Merlins, whimsical farmers full of old lore, and small boys with green-apple bellyache, a fine company of companions for any hot August afternoon.

The stargazers came first. I am fond of stargazers, for they laid the foundations for astronomy and had an unwitting hand in many of the other sciences. They also evolved the complexities of the calendar, which is a constant challenge to my reason and my sense of order. I never look at the history of the calendar without wasting half a day trying to correlate the various systems, sort out the holidays and correction days, and reconcile the lunar and solar months.

But it was history, not astronomy, that rallied the stargazers this day, the history of dog days. It goes back to the early

Romans, and in a sense to the Egyptians and Babylonians too. Rome, of course, was hot and humid at this time of the year. People fell sick and died, dogs ran frothing through the streets, and vipers were quick to bite, often with fatal consequences. Nobody seems to have blamed inadequate sanitation for dysentery and typhoid fever, nobody knew much about rabies, and probably only rural folk knew that snakes shed their skins and are temporarily blind and short tempered about now. Mysterious and malign forces were thought to control life, and among those mysterious forces, thanks to the high priests and stargazers, were the stars and planets. So the official stargazers were ordered to search the heavens for the source of these untoward seasonal happenings.

The stargazers looked and, even as the Greeks and Babylonians before them, found that the star they called Canicula, the Dog Star, was in conjunction with the sun. Obviously, then, Canicula was to blame. And since they couldn't do any more about the movement of the stars than we can today, they fixed the blame on Canicula, said that this was a direful season, and calculated its dates. *Dies Caniculares,* the dog days, ran from July 3 through August 11. Beware, they said, and make sacrifices to the Dog Star.

Thus did the dog days originate, among the stars, not among the cur dogs that prowled the Roman streets. And, since many of our traditions came from Rome, the dog days persist, a time of poisonous ponds, mad dogs, and blind snakes. Had our traditions come from Egypt, the dog days would have a wholly different connotation. In Egypt the Nile rose in flood about the time the Dog Star rose in conjunction with the sun. The Nile's annual flood brought rich silt to Egypt's river bottom fields and was the source of their agricultural plenty. So the Egyptians, who probably also knew sickness and mad dogs and blind snakes at that time, celebrated the dog days and thanked the Dog Star, which they knew as Sirius. If our beliefs had come from Egypt instead of Rome, we might have Thanksgiving Day in August, or even start the new year then, as the Egyptians did.

I never knew anyone to be poisoned by swimming in a scummy August pond, I haven't seen a rabid dog in years, and the records show that more people die of bee stings than snakebites. But the myths persist. Of such flimsy threads are our folkways woven.

The stagnant ponds do look poisonous now, with their algae scum and their myriads of squirming life. Actually, their water is no more poisonous than any stagnant, turbid water. But there is poison in them, or was until we traced the source of malaria and yellow fever and found that certain mosquitoes are their carriers. A century ago the steamy wetlands were believed to have their own miasma that mysteriously engendered the shaking miseries. Out of that circumstance arose the superstition that night air was dangerous. It was, of course, but only because it was full of malarial mosquitoes.

Now we know, but I still hear it said, even by some educated people, that the steamy breath of August over a swamp is dangerous to breathe. I have even heard it said that pond fish won't bite during dog days because "there's something in the air." True, the fish don't bite; but it is because of something in the water, not in the air. The water teems now with larvae and wigglers of all kinds struggling to achieve their final molt and escape into the air on wings. The fish are stuffed to the gills with the most tasty of all natural fish food. Why should they be attracted to the angler's hook?

The swarming mosquitoes, flies, and midges over the boglands, evident now to anyone with eyes to see, explain the flights of swallows and night hawks there in late afternoon and early evening. A countryman full of old beliefs tried to tell me only the other day that those birds congregate in such places "because they hatch in the mud." This goes far back, to the belief that swallows hibernated in the mud, like frogs and turtles.They don't, of course, but there is a vestige of the old superstition. They, with the night hawks and other birds that catch insects on the wing, are over the watery places because that is where the air is full of insects.

And that also explains the glitter of dragonfly wings over the boglands these hot afternoons. Dragonflies, too, seine the air for insect fare and eat mosquitoes by the hundred.

The dragonflies are another part of the August mythology, and they take me back to boyhood, when country folk called dragonflies "snake feeders" and "snake doctors" and "devil's darning needles" and "horse stingers." There was, in fact, a whole volume of dragonfly lore, and remembering it now I am prowling the countryside with barefoot companions and stopping here and there to listen to small-town sages who had more misinformation about nature than even the superstitious boys who questioned them.

"Go swimming during dog days and a devil's darning needle will sew your ears shut."

"Snake feeders catch bugs and give them to hungry snakes."

"A snake doctor can cure a sick snake, even bring a snake back to life after you've stomped its head, just as long as there's a wiggle in its tail."

"Don't ever let one of them horse stingers light on a horse! It'll sting the horse to death."

Actually, dragonflies by any name are as harmless as butterflies, have no "stingers," and want nothing to do with snakes, sick or well, since a snake would as soon eat a dragonfly as look at it. But dragonflies are, in a way, ominous looking, with their long bodies, their metallic-glistening wings, and their huge eyes. And their insistent curiosity can be disconcerting. I never go fishing in mid-Summer without having a dragonfly come to see what I am about. It will circle my head, light on my rod, even perch on my hand and stare at me. I know that dragonflies are utterly harmless, but I wince at their touch and feel uncomfortable when they sit and seem to glare at me. Probably it is the old superstitions still dogging my memory, though there may be another factor too. I know that dragonfly fossils have been found in Paleozoic rocks 300 million years old, remains of dragonflies almost identical with those of today but vastly bigger, some with two-foot wingspread. When a dragonfly perches on my hand and stares at me, I sometimes feel that I, and all my kind, am being appraised by a form of life that has every right to consider man a mere upstart, an experimental creature that has been here only a million years or so. Such a thought is rather disconcerting, even more so than the superstitions.

The apple man demonstrated another degree of superstition, and the fact that he came during dog days was in a sense coincidence. But that morning a couple of boys came past, taking a shortcut to the lake, saw me in the garden, and asked if they could have a couple of green apples. I said yes, of course, but added the warning that green apples caused cholera morbus. They had never heard the term, probably thought I had made it up, and laughed as they went on, eating green apples. I doubt that they got cholera morbus, which is gastroenteritis and can conceivably be caused by eating unripe apples. But boys have stomachs that a billy goat might envy, and in any case I suspect that the warning, which came out of my own boyhood, originated with some farmer who wanted to scare young pilferers away from his apple trees. The term does have a properly awesome sound, though.

A few hours later the apple man arrived. He was a casual acquaintance who lives in the Shenandoah Valley, grows apples for the market, and was on a vacation trip up this way. He stopped to see this valley and this place.

Since he was an apple grower, I asked about the crops down where he lives. And I wondered if the orchardists had trouble with small boys. He didn't understand my question, so I elaborated. But the idea of eating a green apple struck him as wholly senseless. "Green apples," he said firmly, "aren't *good* to eat. You can cook them, but they shouldn't be eaten raw."

"Boys didn't know that, when I was young," I said.

"They do now," he said. "Apples are a business."

"My trees," I said, "are the kind boys like."

"What do you mean by that? What kind are they?"

"Old trees. The kind you can lie under and listen to the birds. And eat green apples."

He smiled, but he didn't understand. "I'd like to have a look at your trees," he said.

So we went around the house and looked at my old trees. He frowned and shook his head. "They need pruning. They're much too tall. How do you pick them?"

"I don't keep them for fruit," I said. "I keep them for the blossoms. The apples are more of a nuisance than anything else. They give us far more apples than we can use, so the deer and other wild animals get most of them."

"How often do you spray?" he asked.

"I don't spray."

"You get a lot of drops, then."

"Sure they drop. So what? I said we don't keep them for the fruit."

"You get wormy apples," he announced.

"That's right, some of them are wormy. Worms have to live too."

He looked at me with a smile and shook his head again. "You aren't an apple man."

"Definitely not. We make a little apple jelly and put up apple sauce to go with roast pork, and we eat all we want of them in season. Beyond that, the apples don't mean a thing to me. But I do like apple blossoms. You should see these trees in May."

"Down my way," he said, "we grow apples for market. Spray them regularly, prune them, keep them low. But," he admitted, "apples haven't got the flavor they used to have, not even our apples."

"I wondered if you would get around to that."

"It's true. I have to admit it. We've bred the apples up, made them pretty to look at, put more color on them. We've made them uniform in size and developed better keeping quality. Now we ship them all over the country. But I wish I'd come when your apples are ripe. I'll bet they have the old-time flavor."

"Quite a bit of flavor," I agreed. "That Snow Apple tree, for instance. And those two Winesaps. They are the old strain."

He picked up a small, green, immature apple from the grass. He looked at it and I knew he was tempted to taste it, sour as it was. But he resisted, maybe remembering the cholera morbus warning from his own boyhood. He looked at it and he said, "My grandfather had a place over along the Hudson, in New York State. I used to go there every Summer, the end of August. Every farmer had his own apple orchard then, and Grandfather had his own cider press. He made his own cider and vinegar, and crocks of apple butter. And when a farm boy wanted a little pocket money, he took a gunny sack and filled it with apples and went to town and peddled them, door to door. Got a quarter, maybe as much as half a dollar, for them. The apples were bruised and some of them were wormy, but that's the way apples were in those days." He sighed. "Apples weren't a business then."

I told him this place had a big orchard, years ago, probably about the time he was talking about. But the trees grew old and the man who owned the place before I bought it had the orchard cut down and sowed to grass, and now it is what we call the home pasture. "But somebody had the good sense to leave a few of the old trees out in the pasture and here in what is now the back yard."

He looked at the trees again, and from the look on his face I knew that he had dismissed those Summers on his grandfather's farm. He was an apple man again. "You could still grow good, marketable apples on these trees," he said, "if you would prune them hard and spray them."

"I don't want marketable apples," I said. "If I had good apples I'd have to pick them, pack them, store them, sell them. I'd have to build a storage place, find markets—no, I don't want to get into the apple business."

"You could make cider," he suggested.

"If I made cider, even if I didn't try to sell it, I would have to make vinegar. And I would want to make some stone fence, as they used to call it. Applejack has its merits, but you can't drink more than a few gallons a year. Try to sell it and you've got revenue officers after you. No, I don't want to make cider. Besides, these aren't very good cider apples."

"No. I guess not. You know what I'd do if I had this place? I'd set out young Macs and Red Delicious trees, and when they started bearing I'd cut down these old trees."

"I don't particularly like Macs or Delicious."

"They sell well. They pay for their keep."

"Apple blossoms are all the payment I want."

He shook his head. "You can't sell apple blossoms, and you can't eat them."

"I can look at them."

He didn't seem to hear. He wanted to make me rich, I guess. "You could keep bees," he said. "Apple blossoms make good honey, and after the blossoms are gone you've got clover in your pastures, I see. You could even plant a field of buckwheat. With a few hives of bees——"

"I've got a swarm of bees," I told him. "Wild bees. They live in a hollow in that big sugar maple in front of the house."

"They make a lot of honey? Wild honey brings a premium price."

"Do you think I would cut down that maple just to get a few pails of honey?" I asked.

"No," he conceded, "I guess not." And he gave up. He came back to the house, got his hat, said good-bye and drove away.

So this afternoon I have the apple man and his mythology about the purposes of apple trees to think about, along with the Roman stargazers and the poisonous ponds and the swallows and the dragonflies. And if I weren't so comfortably August-lazy, so content with the dog-days world around me, I might undertake a serious examination of some of the more obvious myths and superstitions in the theory and practice of commercial economics. The belief that everything must pay its way in dollars and cents, for instance. Or that more and more always means better and better.

I have no real quarrel with the apple man, who only wanted to make me rich when all I wanted was to smell the perfume and see the beauty of apple blossoms. He was a practical man, and the theories of utility and profit that he subscribes to are an essential part of the myths underlying any commercial culture. The only difficulty is that we constantly exalt such mythologies to the status of gospel, the one and only living truth, and insist that everyone embrace them. My apple-growing friend would have me plant new, profitable trees and cut down my old ones. Or make and market cider. Or set the bees to work for me. Anything to make a dollar. And that is where we part company. I appreciate dollars, and even respect them; but I know there are some things on which no one can set a dollar value. The superstition about the universal necessity of a profit motive takes its place, in my mind, with the superstition about dog days.

Goodness knows, we need myth and even superstition. Without them we would have no dreams nor any belief in anything beyond ourselves. But now and then we should pause and examine the myths and appraise them. Our strangely scrambled cultures seem always to be based on an incredible mixture of truth and nonsense, and the wonder is not that so many foolish superstitions survive but that we have rid ourselves of some of them. We no longer really believe the dog-days myth. We know about malaria and rabies and snake venom. And we know that apple blossoms make little green apples, and little green apples grow into big, red, marketable apples. Someday we may get around to suspecting the validity of some of the current superstitions about the omnipotence of statistics and the infallibility of data. We may even find that people are people, with all their individual differences, not items in a census report or dots on a population chart.

Meanwhile we struggle along, embracing one myth after another and trying to impose them on each other. Threatening small boys who eat green apples with the ghastly-sounding cholera morbus. Threatening ourselves with industrial and financial disaster if we fail to buy more than we need and waste more than we use.

We may be, as we sometimes boast, on our way to ultimate truth about life and a lot of other things. But it is just possible that we are merely rationalizing our knowledge up to this point. We tend to mistake facts and documentation for knowledge, and we cling to the age-old habit of mistaking documented myth for truth. After all, facts are tools, not an end in themselves. Man is a biased witness in explaining any form of life, and the most biased of all possible witnesses when it comes to human life. Perhaps we are in an age of fact-blindness. Perhaps we can believe only the myths we constantly create.

All I know at this point is that the old stargazers were as sure as we are that they had the the key to ultimate truth. They didn't, of course, and I doubt that we have. But those old boys who believed in astral reasons for the dog days are not unwelcome companions, even today. They knew a good deal about the stars, which are an enduring mystery. The stars are still here, and I am here, and we both belong to the universe, whether I know ultimate truth and reason or not. I am quite sure that their mystery, and mine, will not be solved tomorrow; but it is comforting to have such mysteries in my cosmos. It makes me, as a sentient being aware of the mystery itself, somewhat a part of the whole mythology of life, along with the birds and bees and dragonflies, even with the serpents that molt and have short, poisonous tempers. We are all in this, whatever it is, together.

5

HARVEST AND THE FORGOTTEN
GODS

September is the month of the Autumnal equinox, and although we always begin it with August's leftovers we end it with Fall creeping in quiet as morning mist, brilliant as a maple leaf, bold as the hoot of a barred owl in the light of the harvest moon. First frost probably will come, and we will be fortunate; our garden, thanks to the river that flows close by, will be spared for another week or two. But the growing season is practically over now. We have been harvesting already, even while the late sweet corn matures, and soon we will be digging late beets and carrots for storage, bringing in the Winter squashes, and gathering green tomatoes and cabbages for one more batch of piccalilli. The parsnips will wait in the ground till after the first hard frost, which somehow sweetens them. But I have already begun to redd up the garden for Winter and next year's planting.

That is the way of life on the land. You don't merely close out one season and say, "That's that." You look forward to another year; which is a way of telling yourself that there is a continuity, an inevitable progression, one year to the next. "Harvest" is a very old word that stems back to herbs, the growing things that were here long before man came to harvest them. And that is something to remember in the time of maturity and falling leaves. Man didn't invent the harvest; he merely found that he could profit by it, and he still does.

Fall and harvest are natural consequences that reach back beyond the time of man, to a time when the land itself was rising from the depths and the ooze was pregnant with potentialities of myriad forms of life and growth. Perhaps it is significant that both words, "Fall" and "harvest," have Germanic origins that long predate the Norman Conquest. They go back to a time when all men were close to the land and knew intimately such matters as cause and effect. That knowledge was not complete, and it was overlaid with what we call superstition. Men knew that you had to plant if you would reap, but they also believed that unless you propitiated the gods of harvest you probably faced a long, hard, hungry Winter. Man, in those days, was in league with the land, but he was at the mercy of the gods.

Over the centuries, man has grown away from the land and disowned the gods. Those gods, at least, the old gods. He has displaced them with the modern gods of statistics and mathematical probabilities, and now he is at the mercy of the machines that calculate those probabilities. But somehow Autumn continues to lure man back to the land, if only on outings to see the brilliant foliage and the Autumn hills. And there, on occasion, he is uneasily aware of the forgotten gods. Not often, but from time to time. As we are who still live close to the land and participate directly in the harvest.

Only the other day one of my farmer neighbors, discussing the year as we tend to do each Fall, spoke of his short hay crop.

We had a severe drouth in my area and many farmers had to cut corn intended for grain to fill their silos. Charley spoke of his short hay crop and the corn he sacrificed to his silo, and he said, "I guess we just don't live right. But maybe we can do better next year." And there was the venerable harvest-god belief paired with the insistent farmer belief. The harvest-god reference was jocular and oblique, following ancient form, but it acknowledged a god who punished and rewarded. The reference to another year, another chance, was typical of the countryman's belief in tomorrow.

When I examine my own beliefs I find a degree of reverence but little piety. There are gods of life and growth and harvest in my cosmos, and there is the great, inexorable force, the pattern of the universe; but my attitude toward them is one of deep, abiding respect rather than worship. A living, growing creature myself, I feel that I partake of all these forces in some measure and I am grateful to be a part of them, to be alive; but I find it difficult to enshrine them and impossible to abase myself before them. I abide by their decrees, insofar as I am aware of them—if I were to refuse, this life I treasure would immediately be in hazard; but beyond that I find it impossible to go. Beyond that, the choice is mine. It is as simple as that.

I am sure it would be easier and more reassuring if I could consolidate and personify these matters, if I could feel the presence of one god as personal as a father. But fatherhood is a biological function, not necessarily a source of either omniscience or omnipotence. My gods are forces, not fathers, and they live and have their being right here among us. I acknowledge their demands, which add up to the necessities of my existence.

Charley made his reference, unwitting though it was, to the harvest gods, and I raised no questions. And he went on to talk about how he plowed and fertilized and planted, and how one field did better than another despite the drouth. And that, too, was a part of the harvest—the recapitulation. You can't live with plants that depend on the sun and the rain and lean with the wind without seeing that there are forces beyond the eager reach of man's hand. Maybe it is disappointing to admit that no law on the statute books ever fended off a late Spring frost or an early Fall freeze, and that neither cutworms nor chinch bugs have yet been legislated out of existence. But it is something worth pondering. We hatch eggs in an incubator, and we ripen tomatoes, of a sort, in a greenhouse in mid-Winter; but man has yet to learn how to create so humble and effective an element of life as an onion bulb. Even the scientists, who in their own way and by their own admission are among the most powerful of men, can't do that. It takes a seed or another bulb to do it, and it takes soil and sunlight and rain, which are rather fundamental matters. It requires the presence of those forgotten gods.

But even those approachable gods, as I think of them, make demands, which I spoke of only a moment ago as necessities. If I would participate in even so inevitable a matter as the seasons and their consequences I must be, myself, involved. I must be engaged in such things. I suspect that this is best explained by examining its opposite, disengagement.

I first heard that word, "disengagement," in this sense when a group of young men and women came up here a few weeks ago for a country weekend. They abided by the amenities, but only within the bounds of cool reserve. They took little part in any conversation and no part in discussion of ideas or events. They did only their small part in the necessary chores of the day and their attitude seemed to be a kind of polite "So what?" But at last one of them answered a direct question by saying, "You don't seem to understand that we are disengaged. *You* settle things, if you think you can. We'll wait and see."

And there it was, disengagement. They had abdicated to some kind of inanimation, trying to ignore even the flow of life and the world around them. This was their world, yet they disowned it. Or was it their world? Perhaps not, since this world belongs, if that is the term, to those willing to be engaged, to accept the challenge of reality.

Man has always faced two fundamental challenges—the land and the weather. The land represents work and the weather represents comfort, even survival. Master those two challenges and all that is left is man against man, or eventually man against his machines. Every civilization of which we have record lost its momentum when its challenges were reduced to that stage.

Nobody in his right mind will try to argue that farm life, intimately dependent on the challenges of land and weather, represents the ultimate of civilization. It is debatable whether life in urban centers, remote from the land and to a considerable degree possessed of artificial weather, does either if you believe, as I do, that humanity as well as learning and enlightenment are essential to the civilized state. But life close to the land does involve, even demand, engagement, participation, and a degree of the larger understanding. Call it awareness of the forgotten gods, if you will.

Living with the land, I am forced to respect those gods as well as the land itself. I am constantly reminded that food doesn't actually grow in a supermarket. I know that weather is not something invented and manufactured in the Weather

Bureau and parceled out day by day. I know how long it takes an oak tree to grow, and a maple. I know that too much rain causes floods and too little rain causes drouths and failing wells and springs. I know the dimensions of the day, the seasons, the years.

Are these important things to know? Yes. Knowing them, I am a part of elemental matters; and being a part, I absorb as with the air I breathe a degree of patience and perspective. I cannot refuse to be engaged, by the very nature of where I live and how I live. Even if I lived on wild nuts and berries and never turned a furrow or planted a seed, I should still be engaged. I am engaged, participating, every day and every hour.

Inevitably, I am aware of the basic challenges of land and weather, though I try to keep from open conflict with either of them. I, too, like my ease and comfort. But a good part of that comfort comes from knowing that there are other challenges than those of man to man, more enduring challenges than those of the machine. None of us knows all the answers, but if there are answers I am sure they will not be flashed on any computer's panel at the push of a button. They will be deliberated, and they will take into account some of the things I am here on the land to learn and understand. Otherwise they will not be answers at all, but only temporizing words.

We are wordy creatures, we featherless, two-legged animals, able to rationalize anything we wish to do or avoid doing. Being by nature lazy, we long ago established the myth that work is a curse laid upon mankind by an offended god. But the high priests, who were ex-officio tribal leaders aware of political necessities, softened the curse into a commandment and persuaded their followers that they could build an Eden with their own hands and sweat. Thus were frontiers tamed and wildernesses made habitable. And whether the wilderness became his Eden or not, man found that with sufficient work he could eventually achieve a semi-godhood of his own. He at least achieved the power to dominate his environment to a large degree, to build comfort and security.

Then another breed of high priests arose and created a whole new theology called Science. They spoke a new language largely composed of symbols and equations, but their basic doctrine was really very old. Work again was called a curse. And, having achieved a kind of Eden with the sweat of his own brow, man was now promised heaven itself. Machines would do the work and man could lie on a foam-rubber cloud, turn a dial for music, hot or cool, and live forever in a balmy atmosphere of ease with only the whirr of hidden machines to remind him of labor.

That was easy to rationlize and accept. But in doing so we missed one vital point. As long as man lived in his self-created Eden he was somewhat in control and thus partook of at least demi-godhood. Now, living in heaven, he had abdicated not only his power but his godhood to the machines. Despite the ancient myth, power is a consequence of work and a basic element of godhood. Even in the old mythology, God labored to create the universe. He didn't leave it to chance or some super-atomic force. And in the lesser mythologies the various gods do not sit back and spend all their time sipping nectar on an air-conditioned mountaintop. They are right down here tending to the fall of rain, the flow of rivers, the sprouting of seed, the ripening of grain, and the welfare of whatever happens to be their personal responsibility. They do the jobs that somebody has to do to keep things going.

This is a roundabout and perhaps whimsical way of getting

at some of the truths inherent in this matter of engagement. But it is the primary reason I find it good to be here at the root of enduring matters, where engagement is inevitable.

This afternoon I set out with my dog to see how the rabbits fare and if the partridges are doing all right on my mountainside. But as I walked the pasture edges I saw that industry and a measure of dispute with nature were again a necessary part of my engagement here, conditions of my tenancy. There was a flash of sumac war bonnets creeping down a swale in the lower pasture. If we don't check that sumac this Winter we shall lose another acre or so of ladino and brome grass. We have fought that sumac steadily, and all we seem able to do is hold it at bay.

Then I remembered the day last week when I pulled half a hundred maple seedlings out of a corner of the flower garden where the wind had lodged a drift of ripe keys. They came out easily, but if I had left them they would have become a thicket of saplings that in another ten years would have had us camping in the woods. They were seedlings from the big maples we tap now and then, for sap to make syrup and sugar. But I can't let them take over the flower garden, fond as I am of the parent trees. Down the road is a field that was good corn land less than ten years ago. It was neglected for a few years, then abandoned to weeds and seedlings, and now it is a thicket without even a blade of grass. A beautiful thicket when all those sumac and ash and maple and birch leaves turn gold and scarlet, but a thicket just the same.

Pat, the dog, ran a few rabbits on the mountainside, and I put up partridges from almost every clump of barberry the birds have planted up there, and we came back to the house, both of us pleased with the state of our world. There were rabbits to run, partridges to hunt, and provender from the cultivated land. And we were here to enjoy the fruits of the season. Maybe that is why Fall seems so important. One season's work is done. Now there will be time for other, less strenuous tasks, and time to think, to feel, quietly to live.

I contemplate the total harvest and feel as full of achievement as a gray squirrel who has made good his personal claim to a big butternut tree full of ripe, sweet nuts. Maybe more so, because I had a hand—only a hand, because my harvest really was governed by the weather and the soil—in the planting and the tilling. The squirrel, being an inferior creature, planted at random and without particular purpose. I doubt that he knows that some of the nuts he hides and fails to recover and eat eventually will sprout and grow into trees that will bear more nuts long after he is dead and forgotten. Since I presume the squirrel to have only a limited memory, his knowledge of rather remote cause and current effect must also be limited. He certainly didn't plant the butternut tree he now harvests, though one of his ancestors may have. So mine is the more intelligent pleasure. Or so I think, needing the superior feeling to which man, a superior being, is entitled; the feeling of intelligent planning brought to fruitful conclusion.

Of course, when we get in the car and travel a bit, even here in this area, I see a natural harvest on a scale that makes my own efforts seem inconsequential. There is a harvest on every hill, in every woods and swamp. But it would be treason for me to admit this too generally. Man is the creature who does this kind of thing, isn't he? Man is the master in these matters. It is man's world, and he is constantly telling himself that he knows best and does best at shaping his own environment. Why, man can even make the desert to blossom as the rose!

Of course he can. He makes the deserts bloom. He also

creates new deserts. He builds dams, diverts rivers, cuts trees, drains swamps. Man is the master of big achievements. But they really aren't a fraction as big as the quiet achievement of grass taking over again and healing the scars after man's flocks and his ill-advised plows have created a dust bowl, or as of timber eventually renewing itself after man's saws and axes have denuded a thousand wooded hills.

Man can do many things, do them on a tremendous scale—tremendous by his own measure. But an ice sheet, a flood, a slight shift in the winds that bring rain clouds, can do more to change the land in one season than a dozen generations of men. When I travel the land, whether in New England or the Midwest or the South or the Far West, anywhere, I see a land still essentially shaped by forces beyond the human hand or brain, a land that can still hide the man-made cities among its hills. And I wonder why man, with all his talk and management and planning, has so much trouble managing himself. Half the energy and imagination he expends on trying to manage the earth would suffice to ease, if not wholly solve, the most galling of our man-to-man problems.

Somehow the natural environment asserts itself more fully in the Fall than at any other time of the year, perhaps because it reveals its own strength of creation and fulfillment then. Man is only an inhabitant of the land, a beneficiary of natural forces. But when he goes forth in the Fall and sees what has been happening he too often says, "See what I have wrought! See my great accomplishment!"

As though he could color ten million maple and sour gum and sassafras leaves, or fashion a pumpkin in a laboratory, or create electronically the voice of a fox on a September hillside in the moonlight. As though he had built the mountains, which can dwarf his biggest dams and hide them in a lesser canyon. As though he could fashion so simple a thing as a cumulus cloud in the blue September sky.

The world is putting on its finery now, its harvest finery, the triumphant colors of fruition. The forgotten gods are smiling and the shape of the earth, the home of perhaps transient man, begins to clarify. Fall winds are blowing, clearing the air. Frost will soon skip down the valleys, precursor of snow and Winter, of another Spring and another new beginning.

If the year holds any one moment when man is urged to go forth and appraise his own works and weigh their consequence, this surely is that time. How old are the pyramids? Less than six thousand years. And that maple down the road, the one that in another two or three weeks will be a shimmering flame of pink and gold, was an ancient species when the Egyptians were still abysmal savages. How long has man ground meal and cooked bread? Perhaps 50,000 years, perhaps even longer. But the wheat from which we make today's bread, and even the rye and barley of ancient bread, grew as a wild grass literally as old as the hills when man was first experimenting with a flint tip for his hunting spear. That stream flowing down to the sea was a child of the ice age when man had not yet learned to hollow a log and fashion a boat with which to cross its current.

Now is the time for man to look and learn. Perhaps when he has reaped another ten thousand harvests he will know that it is himself, not the earth, that challenges his genius as a dreamer and a doer and calls for management. Perhaps he will learn that there are still gods of the hills and fields, of life and growth and harvest who, if they do no longer demand propitiation, do call for recognition.

6

AUTUMN ON THE RIDGE

For anyone who lives in the oak-and-maple area of New England there is a perennial temptation to plunge into a purple sea of adjectives about October. The more laconic natives, especially those not in the tourist business, speak of "the color" and let it generate its own superlatives; but I am not quite that laconic, being a word-man by trade. For the moment, however, I will say only that even a color-blind person must now be glad to be alive and able to get outdoors. I went out for an hour the other morning and came back reluctantly. Even the best ordered of human habitations now seems dull and prosaic. Nature does it so much better, and with so much less obvious effort, that I feel embarrassed.

But as I walked the ridge back of the house and beyond the pastures, I was thinking not only of the color but of the season itself which, even in anthropomorphic terms, is more than a colored leaf, a ripe acorn, or a migrating goose. Autumn is both a corrective and a reminder, and anyone living close to the land or even periodically visiting the country with an open eye and mind must sense this.

One Autumn afternoon an industrial chemist who didn't

know a blue jay from a bluebird walked that ridge with me. The leaves were drifting down like giant gold and crimson snowflakes, and my chemist friend picked up one of them and asked about the process of leaf coloring. We discussed chlorophyll, sugar, and starch, and such pigments as carotene, anthocyanin, and xanthophyll, and he said, "Waste. Sheer waste. The color serves no vital purpose then?"

"That depends," I said, "on what you mean by purpose. There's no vital purpose in the color of a sunset either, I suppose."

"I mean the color doesn't contribute anything to the tree."

"Not much, except beauty."

"The tree could live and grow without the leaf color, couldn't it? The color is just an unnecessary by-product."

"In a sense," I said, "yes. It's a kind of leftover. But the chemicals in the leaves, even the pigments, leach out into the soil and the tree undoubtedly uses them again." And I dug down under the crisp leaves to the maturing leaf mold beneath.

He studied this for a moment, then said, "If we could achieve just one chemical cycle that would feed on its own wastes and build something as substantial as a tree . . ." He shook his head.

And there it was. He had seen the truth in a leaf. He was admitting that while the technicians can extract all kinds of things from wood, turpentine to alcohol, tar to paper, they have to start with a tree. They can't create a tree. All they can do is cut it down and disintegrate it.

I forget who said that if Autumn came only once in ten years we would hold national and international celebrations of the event. There is some truth in that, but not the whole truth. After a few decades we probably would accept a decennial Autumn pretty much as we now do the annual occurrence. The cyclic event loses its distinction and even becomes tiresome with repetition. How often does the average person, even the nature-sensitive person, go out especially to see the full-moon brilliance of the night? There is little novelty in moonlight. It is too common a commodity. Watching the harvest moon a couple of weeks ago, I wondered if the plan to rocket a man to the moon will rouse interest in the moon itself or merely pique a morbid curiosity about the fate of the lunarnaut, or whatever the multibillion-dollar skyrocketeers choose to call him.

But Autumn on my ridge is neither the time nor place to dwell on such human super-pranks. I did spend a few subversive moments wondering how many classrooms and hospital wards could be built for the cost of one moon rocket. Then a couple of gray squirrels, harvesting acorns in a big white oak, chattered indignantly at my intrusion and brought me back to earth and reality. They were storing those acorns for the Winter, driven by the instinct for survival. Fortunately they have no weatherproof warehouses in which to store them, so the excess acorns have a chance to sprout and grow into oaks that will ripen acorns for other squirrels twenty or thirty years hence. Squirrels don't know about such things, but men do. Men are bright about such things. Men are so intelligent that when they grow more wheat and corn than they need they hide it, not where it can grow and feed hungry men tomorrow, but locked away safe from all natural laws except those of rot and mildew. Men now plan to plant a man on the moon for some reason connected with the survival of the human race. I hope they don't forget to send a woman along, if that is actually the reason. Up to now man seems a bit slow in mastering parthenogenesis, though the aphids in my garden which probably can't count up to two achieved parthenogenetic birth a long, long time ago. I'm just reactionary enough to hope they keep their secret.

One thing about my ridge, or any ridge for that matter, is that you get a sense of time and distance up there in October. Time, of course, is an inexplicable dimension in which we all participate but of which no one is master. There is the time of the universe, and the time of the rocks, and the time of man; and about all we have ever done with time is split it into fragments so that we can count the fleeting bits. Achievement of the micro-second hasn't altered the individual life span one iota. I notice that the trees keep right on counting time by years, ring by annual ring, pretty much as the earth tallies time in its own sediments.

Distance is something else again, whether we measure it in light-years or millimeters. Distance is the length of a man's stride and the reach of his eye. It is the height of a mountain and the breadth of a continent or an ocean. It can even be the closeness or the remoteness between two men and two nations and the ideas that dominate their thinking.

The strange thing is that Autumn, especially on a wooded ridge, changes the relationship of time and distance. The days shorten, and at the same time they increase in height and breadth. It is almost as though there were a fixed ratio that keeps the days in balance. The leaves begin to fall and the eye begins to reach. New vistas open. I saw those vistas opening that morning, there on the ridge, and my eye could see brand-new horizons. Not exactly new, of course, since they have been there since this earth assumed its present shape; but they seemed new that morning because they were newly seen after weeks and months when they were hidden. And I know that tonight I can look up from my dooryard, through the branches of the big sugar maples, and see the constellations of Pegasus and Andromeda. They, too, have been there a long time, but I couldn't see them from the dooryard all Summer.

That is what I meant when I said earlier that Autumn is a corrective. It is color and ripeness and a season of natural completion; but it is also a time of breadth and depth and distance annually brought back to our attention. I wonder if anyone can stand on an Autumn hilltop, or out in the dooryard on an October evening, and fail to see the new expanse not only around but in himself too. Autumn is itself a kind of affirmation.

Here at the house the leaves came down last week like snow and the wind blew the wrong way to take them off the grass. There was nothing to do but rake them and put them on the compost heap where they will become leaf mold that I can restore to the garden next Spring. So I raked and lugged the leaves in a tarp over my shoulder, and the more I raked and the more I lugged, the more certain I became that I was participating in Autumn's affirmation. In that simple task I was affirming my belief in matters that are being challenged day after day. Particularly my belief in a tomorrow, a future. In survival, if you will, despite all the mushroom clouds, figurative as well as literal, about which we are constantly warned.

Raking leaves and building a compost heap isn't much of a gesture, really. As far as I am concerned, it isn't a gesture at all. It is just a way of life. But it is affirmation, of a kind, and if anyone wants to think of it as a gesture, I say that it is the little gestures, the daily routines, that are more important

than the loud words and the big defiances. And the more I
thought of this, raking those leaves, the more certain I was
that most of us are doing those quiet, affirmative things without thinking of them as important beyond the ordinary. We
live our belief, our fundamental belief, as we go about our
daily routines.

But that aspect of life seldom makes headlines, though in
the big picture of events I am sure it is the most dramatic story
of today. It just doesn't sound dramatic coming out of a radio
or a television set, and it doesn't look dramatic in print to say
that millions of people expect the sun to rise tomorrow and
Thanksgiving and Christmas to come on schedule and the
earth to turn green and bountiful again next Spring. And who
ever would think it was headline news that I was raking
leaves?

But those are the big, important facts. And they certainly
don't add up to a refusal to face reality. Reality is the long
story of mankind, quarrels and everything else, wars and
truces and times of peace, hope and despair and failure and
achievement. And belief persisting.

As I loaded the tarp again and carried another load of
leaves to the compost heap I weighed that word, "belief." What
do we believe in, anyway? Well, we believe in certain fundamental values, human values. We believe in freedom of mind
and spirit, and in a degree of perfectibility of life, if not of
human nature. We believe in excellence. We believe in love,
and in charity of spirit, and in truth. We believe in knowledge
and the search for understanding. We haven't always lived up
to the ideals of our belief, but in the final judgment of such
matters we have usually tried to do what seemed right. As a
people, we have, and largely as individuals. We still get lost,
from time to time, and we probably always will. We tolerate

82

the cult of the anti-hero and we put up with the recurring foolishness of the moral anarchists. But as long as we know there is imperfection we are aware of perfection.

None of this is wholly new. We didn't invent things to believe in. They were here, and we accepted them, tried to live by them most of the time. We sometimes speak of such matters as the Judeo-Christian ethic, but the basis goes further back than that. The Golden Rule was stated, with only slight variations, in most of the earliest religions and philosophies of which we have record. So was the substance of the Sermon on the Mount. Mankind climbed out of the pits of ancient savagery on such ladders of belief.

The wind blew my leaves and I had to start raking all over again, and I thought of all the people in Europe and Asia and Africa who were out raking leaves, or doing something just as normal. I thought of the interminable speeches by bombastic men who threaten and bully and yet find time to promise pie in the sky in some tomorrow. Even they seem to think there will be someone around to eat that pie. And I thought of people all over the world getting married and building houses, begetting children and sending them to school, plowing fields, planting, harvesting food, just as though they knew there was going to be a next year.

Why don't our dramatic voices and hot typewriters get around to those people, even in a minor way? Why don't they stop thinking of international relations like a world series or a football game that can be won by a home run or a blocked punt? I wish the sports writers would go back to sports and let the statesmen handle their own business, and ours, for a change. It might be a good thing if the generals and admirals got back to their own business too. I wondered if they ever raked leaves.

Then I thought of a little band of foreigners, bedraggled newcomers, on the Massachusetts coast 300-odd years ago. They probably had a few folk around telling them that if the Indians didn't scalp them they would die of disease in another fortnight or two. But the way I read the story, most of them patched the roof and brought in the pumpkins and salted down a few cod. If there had been lawns they probably would have raked leaves when the other daily tasks were done. Instead, they cut wood and wove cloth. Such tasks are never done and ended, and doing them seems to be an old, old habit of mankind.

I was thinking of these things up on the ridge the other morning, and before I came down to the valley and back to the house I climbed to the crest where the backbone of the hills in this part of the world lies open and exposed. There is something of a jumble of rocks up there, and few trees of any consequence. At the very crest is a huge, table-like rock, weathered and gray and patched with lichen. The rock is mostly quartzite and marble, with some mica schist. The quartzite is a metamorphosed sandstone, in geologic terms, hard and durable. The marble is a form of limestone and somewhat softer. The weather has worn away the marble faster than it has worn the quartzite, but the lichen is slowly eating into the intractable harder rock.

I stood there looking at the patches of lichen, like miniature gray and green maps of imaginary places, and I remembered my surprise when I first learned that lichens are dual plants living in symbiosis, a fungus and an alga, neither of which could exist in such a place alone. The fungus collects moisture and the alga manufactures food. Each does its job and together they persist in this difficult evironment where either would perish by itself. The lichen not only persists but flourishes, slowly wearing away the rock and building little patches of soil. Moss was growing in some of those patches, grass in others, and I even found a small red cedar in one patch where there was a deeper accumulation of soil than elsewhere.

I turned and came down the slope, watching those new horizons through the thinning leaves, admiring the purple tinge of viburnum leaves and the deep crimson of blueberry. It was a vivid world and I must say that "the color" is quite inadequate to describe it. It was a magnificent world, full of gold and scarlet and tan and brown, and every shade of red I ever knew. And the sky was a depth of blue it seems never to achieve except in October.

I came on down the hillside, and the farther I came the more I wondered why the political leaders who hold this world's critical decisions in their hands don't meet for a conference on such a hillside at this season of the year. The more I considered this idea, the more persuaded I became that people, and especially those who make the big and fateful decisions, have worked themselves into a serious case of cabin fever. If you don't know that term, cabin fever is a state of nerves achieved by men who have been confined too long in a small cabin, usually in the depth of Winter. They become so suspicious and so resentful of each other that they often commit mayhem, sometimes murder.

Nobody ever got cabin fever on an open hilltop in October.

I don't know why, but it is the long-time habit of our leaders to hold their crucial conferences within four walls. Manmade walls. It is as though they were afraid to face the dimensions of time and distance and must roof themselves away from the eternities of the sky. There they deliberate what may well be the fate of man, all men.

Approaching the far side of my home pasture, which is now showing a touch of bronze and wholly beautiful, I wondered why there shouldn't be an Autumn conference on such a hilltop as mine. With a rock for a conference table, a rock already equipped with maps of a possible tomorrow. Lichen-maps, which are living, growing examples of symbiosis, of two separate elements of life that thrive in mutual give and take. A council seated around such a rock, with the glory of Autumn all around. Perhaps the light and air of the season would ventilate not only the mind and thinking but the problems themselves which, after all, are man-made problems. It might work, particularly if the generals and the admirals were left behind, for once, out of earshot. It might.

I came on across the pasture and through the gate to the orchard and back yard. There were so many leaves on the grass where I raked them just the other day that I was tempted to get the rake and the tarp and go to work again. But the shimmering beauty of the sugar maples made me stop in my tracks and try to drink it all in, as I have been drinking every day for two weeks. If it were wine I should be roaring drunk by now, and not give a damn what happened.

I was still standing there when my neighbor down the road drove up and saw me and stopped and shouted, "What do you see up there?"

"A tree," I said. "A sugar maple that's so rich it's throwing away gold coin by the truckload."

Albert grinned. "Talk that way, they'll make you report it on your income tax."

"If they do," I said, walking over to his car, "I'll pay them in kind. I wonder what they'd do if I sent them a bale of maple leaves instead of a bank check." Then I asked where he was going.

"Corn picker broke down," he said. "I've got to get a new part. Need anything I can get for you in the village?"

I said no, and thanked him, grateful for his thoughtfulness. I stood beside his car and we talked a bit, mostly about his corn and the yield he was getting. And suddenly there was a thunderclap in the cloudless sky and we saw a needle-nosed jet, mosquito-small, racing toward the horizon, a contrail in its wake.

Albert shook his head. "I wonder what they're writing up there, what it really means."

I said, "Mene, mene, tekel, upharsin."

"What's that?" Albert asked.

"Just an old saying."

"Well, I've got to get along if I'm ever going to get that corn in the corn house." And Albert drove on, toward the village.

I turned and looked at the color on the ridge, and at the stark white contrail in the cloudless sky. And I wished they would come and sit down around that old lichen-covered rock and talk. Right now, today.

7

A TIME FOR SUMMARY

The katydids have rasped their last calls of the season, the frogs have hibernated in the mud, the whippoorwills have gone South, and if man would only abide by the season we could settle down to a few weeks of peace and quiet. November brings that pause between Summer and Winter when a man should be able to listen to his own thoughts and call a truce in the noisy war with his environment.

Up here in the hill country, this area of small but venerable farms, we are catching our breath after tending to such fundamental matters as getting the hay into the mow, filling the silos and stowing the garden's yield in the freezer and the root cellar. The county fair is over. The political campaign has almost run its course. Tomorrow we shall go to the polls and, with luck, the dust will settle and the uproar die down before the first snow flies.

I was up on the mountainside the other afternoon taking a census of the partridges which, in the terse local way, we simply call "birds." I knew the birds had a good season, a big hatch and a profitable Summer. As a countryman, I saw the signs weeks ago. But I was surprised at the number of birds I

flushed from the briar patches and the clumps of wild barberry where they were feeding. Some rocketed from the brush
almost at my feet with a startling roar, and some winged away
in swift silence. A partridge can either scare the wits out of
you or be as quiet as a shadow. There was a time, long ago,
when they were so tame you could knock one over with a short
stick. Now they are wary. You need a shotgun and sharp re-
flexes to get a brace of birds. Partridges learned about man
quite a few generations back. Having learned, they survive.

When I had satisfied myself about the birds, I sat down on a
rock where I could look through an opening among the trees
and see the distant hills and the clean horizon. Sitting there in
the sunlight and the silence, I thought how the world reveals
itself in its true dimensions in the Autumn, how a man's
vision is invited to reach and his understanding to expand.
That thought invited parallels, including the notion that a
man on his way to the polls in early November could, if he
would, look around and see the world in its basic contours,
and the notion that neither men nor issues can hide in the
leafless woods. But these notions were conceits and no doubt
superficial, apt as they seemed at the moment. I dismissed
them and came back to the trees, the far hills, and the scat-
tering of small farms I could identify from where I sat. They
represented something vital, something about mankind and
man's tenure on the earth. They embodied traditions and a
way of life that, up till now, have been a basic pattern in
America.

I had to draw that reservation, that "up till now," because
in the back of my mind was the report, made not long ago, by
an advisory committee surveying national economic factors.
That report examined the infinitely complex farm problem
and recommended that the government solve it by wiping
out more than two and a half million small farms and moving

a whole generation of farm boys off the land and into industry. It was obviously based on statistics and, like most statistical thinking, it ignored many factors that invariably slip through the statistical net, particularly when people are involved. It was another example of the notion that bigness and organization can solve anything and that human problems can be solved by pushing people around. But since we are more and more at the mercy of the statistical thinkers and their machines, that report was like an icy wind blowing out of a dismally regimented tomorrow.

For a few moments, there on the mountainside, my thoughts leaped from human wisdom to human folly, from dreams to failures, from hopes to despairs. Then I felt the sun on my back and smelled the day and let my senses and sensibility tell me that this was good, this was satisfying and reassuring, just to be here on the mountainside in the November afternoon. The year was in order, the rhythms of time and growth and change just as they had been for eons, and I was there to see and know and participate as far as man can ever really participate in such matters. Then I came back to the house to do the evening chores and close out another day in my small segment of time, my own life.

Now, indoors at my desk a few days later, I have the uneasy feeling that I am writing a kind of memoir although I am chronicling events of this moment, this Autumn of the year in the mid-60s of the twentieth century, A.D. I feel somewhat as I felt the other day when we were making repairs to my old barn and I found a strange implement in a pile of rubbish in a far corner of the loft. It was the handle of a flail, and it must have been left there long before I came here. It was a reminder of a time when the farmer who lived here made at least some of his own tools by hand. The hickory haft was fitted with a maple swivel, whittled and steamed to shape long ago. I had never used a flail, nor had the neighbor who was helping me, though he has been a farmer all his life. But somehow, just holding that flail handle and examining its workmanship, both of us participated in the past, in the long tradition of the land. We were, however tenuously, a part of human history.

When I examine the simplicities of this present Autumn, here close to the land, I wonder if I, too, am shaping a flail handle. Perhaps a few years hence, only a few years the way time now races, someone will find these words in a rubbish heap and wonder at them and what they stand for. When I write about trees and birds and the view from a hilltop, I wonder if they are important in the face of the elections, and foreign aid, and taxes, and missiles and satellites. Then I know that arguments end, men die, and nations rise and fall, but that so long as there is an earth and a procession of the seasons there will be trees and birds and vistas from hilltops. And, unless we are all incredibly stupid and recklessly wicked, there will be men here to see these things in Autumn and to feel, if never wholly to understand, what they signify. There will even, I am sure, be men living on the land, planting and reaping and abiding by the land's own ordinances.

So if this should be another flail handle, let it be straight and true to the best of my ability. Let it represent the now and the here that I know.

Any Autumn is the sum of its preceding Spring and Summer. We had a late Spring, but a moist one, followed by a dry, cool Summer. It was what we call "a bug year," insect pests in the garden and voracious inchworms in the woods. Hay was short but haying weather was ideal. Corn was slow but persistent and made a good ensilage crop. Gardens weren't up to par, but the insects ate as many weeds as vegetables. Things balanced out, as they usually do if you give them time.

Up in the woods the worms stripped many trees, and short-term prophets said the woods were doomed unless we aerial-sprayed. Hating all poisons, we put our faith in time and natural controls, remembering similar devastations that failed to kill the trees in ten-year cycles in the past. Only two agencies that I know of have ever been able to strip those hills of their woodland—the ice that came down from the north 10,000 or 12,000 years ago and scoured the land to its very skeleton, and man who came here a mere 300 years ago with his axe, his saw, and his torch. So we refused to let them spray, and the worms ate leaves, stripped quite a few trees. But by August the worms were gone and the woods were green again with a second leafing. I lost no more than half a dozen trees, none of them important trees at that, on the whole mountainside.

September brought an early frost. But we expected it and brought in the garden harvest. When frost came, we were grateful, since no man should be slave to a garden after ripe tomatoes begin to pall on his palate. We cleaned up the garden and called it another job done, another Summer completed, and we had time to watch the color come, first to the woodbine and the sumac, then to the birches and the ash trees, finally to the maples and the oaks. We had time to pick wild grapes and make jelly from them, and to see the milkweed pods begin to burst and glisten the wind with silk, and to marvel at the harvest moon.

Autumn came well before the equinox, and a few days after the equinox the drouth was broken by a long, slow rain that, despite the objections of the meteorologists, we always call the equinoctial storm. We had depended on that storm to come and renew the wells and springs, and when it came we said again that things even out, weather included. As though to demonstrate this, after that storm we had a spell of Indian Summer weather, a series of days when it was good just to be alive.

It wasn't a good year, statistically. But on the land you learn to think in longer terms than one season or one year. Next year probably will be better. But you know that there are bad years as well as good ones, just as there are bad days. You know that even the good years don't come for free, and that in any year you will pay for the long, hot Summer days in the currency of January's short, cold days and February's miserable ones. You know, too, that nobody, not even the United States Senate when it can muster a quorum, can legislate a rain when the corn crop needs it. You learn that nobody, not even the Supreme Court by unanimous vote, can forbid a woodchuck to raid a garden.

Even in a hurrying, impatient world that yearns for quick, easy solutions, the man on the land has patience driven into him by the trees and the grass and every growing thing around him. Long ago it was said, "To every thing there is a season, and a time to every purpose under heaven." Every day of his life, the countryman has that truth impressed upon him. Try as he may, he cannot much alter the seasons or change the sequence of natural purposes. All he can do is attempt to understand these things and work with them. That inevitably tempers the arrogance that has led the human race into so many disasters.

Autumn is a time for summaries, even more so than the end of the calendar year for those who live where the natural world sums up its seasons soon after leaf-fall. The plant summarizes growth in a seed that is pregnant with tomorrow. The tree summarizes another circuit of the sun in a closed circle of fiber that addes to the strength with which it will face the Winter's storms. The insect totals its brief individual life in a cluster of dormant eggs or a cocoon or a hibernating pregnant queen. All of them are implicit with a future, a tomorrow.

Perhaps the summary I have been trying to draw up here has a touch of all these things. To be even approximately complete it should include scarlet leaves and ripened nuts and barking foxes and cloud-high geese honking in the moonlight as they V their way southward with the season. It should be savored with the scent of wood smoke from an open fire and the tang of the pickling kettle in a farm kitchen. It should have the color of moon-size pumpkins and ripe apples and bittersweet berries. Somewhere in it should be the glint of starlight on a moonless night and the glitter of frost at dawn.

And there must be a quiet voice somewhere saying, as a man said to me only a few days ago, "Man and boy, I have lived on this land seventy years, and my father and my grandfather lived here before me. I've sweated and I've froze, I've worked and I've rested, and I've gone hungry a time or two. But never very hungry and never very long. And every Fall I look back and know it's been a good life. What more can a man ask?"

I often wonder about that question. What more can a man ask? Seeking answers, I always come back to the land as I come back now, thinking of that report which would move so many more people away from the land.

Life on the land never was wholly a life of ease, and it still isn't, though in terms of hard work and financial reward it is better today than ever before in history. But a good many of those who have left the land—and this has been true a long, long time—went in search of comfort and leisure and what we call better opportunities. The social philosophers have said over and over that if man could only escape the long hours of exhausting physical labor and the limiting isolation of farm and village life, he woud emerge into the sunlight of a utopia where everyone would be happy, everyone would participate in culture, and the individual would discover identity and flower as a person.

So they left the land, asking ease and leisure. They helped change the pattern of life. In business and industry, they now work forty hours or less a week. Machines do most of the back-breaking work—and at the same time reduce the number of jobs available. But those who work with the machines have more ease and leisure than their grandfathers ever dreamed of, and their standard of living exceeds that of any other people on earth.

But utopia still eludes us.

Mass employment has tended to reduce workers to the functional status of a social insect, and conditions of mass living exert pressures of conformity that only the most rugged can resist. The norm is idealized, the average cherished, and even our education emphasizes adjustment to the ideas and the customs of the group. Leisure has become a problem and boredom is endemic. Young novelists and playwrights, writing as they must from their own experience, hold up a mirror of confusion and pointless search and a confused and rootless audience applauds them.

Searching for a better life, we have created a new and different but not wholly better world. We have eased the burden of labor by abdicating to the machine, which is both mindless and heartless. Analyzing and synthesizing, we have created an incalculable store of materials and things. Factually, we have accumulated vast libraries of technical information about the physical elements of our world. We have in some measure eased the pressures of physical poverty. We have somewhat prolonged life and eased the pain of living.

But a life based on facts and things still leaves largely unanswered the question, "What more can a man ask?" For we have eased want but not destroyed the wanting. We have learned facts, but ultimate causes and reasons still elude us. We have created machines that can answer our questions when we know how to phrase them, but we still haven't learned how to ask the machines why, and where, and what for. In creating this new world, this seedbed for utopia, we have lost and are still losing something vital to us as sentient, living individuals.

So I come back to the land and life upon it. And to specify I must become personal, speak out of my own knowledge.

These things I know:

Fundamentally, man is a minor creature on the face of the earth. I am bigger than a fox but smaller than a cow, and though my life span is longer than that of either fox or cow I, even as they, shall die and disappear in the end. As a species, I am vastly outnumbered everywhere I turn, by the mice, by the grasshoppers, by the birds, even by the frogs and the fish. Yet if I choose I can make the land do my bidding, up to a point and only if I cooperate with the land's own demands. Even without planting a seed or a root I can live off the land, after a fashion. If I cooperate with the soil and the seasons I can produce from the land enough sustenance for perhaps a dozen families. But the choice is mine, to subsist on the land or to produce from it.

If I choose, the land will provide me with shelter, a home. I can live in a cave among the rocks, in a hole in the ground, or in a habitation made of stones or mud or timbers. When I would warm myself, the land provides fuel. When I am thirsty, the land provides water that I can pollute or keep clean, according to my habits—and the habits of my neighbors upstream, of course. For clothing, the land offers fibers and wool and skins that I and my own kind can make into cloth and leather. I have the skills, or can learn them if I am patient, to use what the land offers.

Whether I subsist on the land or prosper here, I will eventually vanish and be forgotten. My footsteps will mark a path across the land, proof of my presence here; but ten minutes after I am gone the grass will grow again where I walked and the rain will smooth the sand where I knelt to plant or to drink. My own kind may remember me for a little while, bless my few acts of kindness, curse my unthinking cruelties, repeat a few of my words; but the fox and the hawk, the maple tree and the briar, will have no recollection of my ever having lived. The moonlight and the rising of the sun will not be altered one iota by my having lived or died.

But while I live I will know sunrise and moonlight, Summer and Winter, growth and harvest. I will watch flowing water and falling snow, and growing grass and nesting birds. I will know beginnings as well as endings, and I will marvel at the progression from egg to worm to butterfly and to egg again, the endless cycle. I will have the chance to participate, to dream, to wonder, and to hope. Not for a better tomorrow any more than for a good today. I will have seen one day after another, no two precisely alike any more than two snow-flakes, though of the same fundamental pattern, are precisely alike.

While I live, I will ask questions. And seek answers in myself, in the world around me, in the skies above. And I shall learn anew each day that answers are sometimes less important than the questioning. I shall continue to believe that facts are not answers, but only the tools with which to fashion more questions. Having experienced fallibility, I shall remain skeptical of omniscience.

Knowing something about the universe as well as the world around me, I resist the temptation to equate change with chaos, proliferation with confusion. Knowing trees, I understand the meaning of patience. Knowing grass, I can appreciate persistence. Knowing skills, I am impatient with mere competence and cherish excellence. Young, I had visions. Old, I shall demand the right to dream.

Thus I come to my own answer to the old man's question.

One more item:

To live with the land is to know, beyond doubt or argument, that change is inevitable. Not even the rocks or the mountains endure forever, so why should one way of life be immutable? My quarrel is not with change but with false prophets. Perhaps the statistical thinkers are right. I doubt it, but if they are, let this be a footnote to their cold, impersonal charts and columns of figures, this report from one man in a rural valley that welcomes another November, another beat in the eternal rhythm that throbs both in the stars and in my own mortal heart.

8

WINTER AND THE HOLINESS

One doesn't have to live in the country to appreciate Winter, but it helps. Winter has many dimensions, and unless one can stand on a December hilltop or walk up a valley stripped to simple fundamentals, one misses some of them. Winter is more than a season bounded by a solstice and an equinox, more even than snowstorms and ice-bound rivers and winds whooping down from the frozen Arctic tundra. It is primitive forces at work, cleansing and scarifying the earth, but it is also beautiful and awesome and full of wonder. It rounds out the year, makes it whole; and, in human terms, it takes the edge off human arrogance at the same time that it makes the country-man proud of his own competence. In a sense, it makes the man who lives with Winter whole again too.

I was out digging parsnips with a pick-axe the other day and looked up at the mountain just beyond the home pasture and thought what a wonderful thing is a mountain, or a pine tree. I even began to wonder if the Indians didn't have an altar up there in the old days. It would be an ideal place to observe the holidays. The Greeks had Mount Olympus, and I have no doubt that the Mahicans who lived here in the valley had a god or two who lived up there on what we unimaginative folk today call Tom's Mountain, or who visited it from time to time to pick up the sacrificial fawns that probably were left there. The Indians knew who made the world and kept it running, and when the sun cut a smaller and smaller arc in the sky and the nights grew longer and longer and colder and colder, they knew that only the gods could do anything about it. So they did what they could to please those gods. We rely on the almanac to handle things like that for us.

I looked up the mountain and saw the white pines and hemlocks, doubly green with their light dusting of snow, and I saw the deep, distant blue of the sky beyond. Of course we have a completely rational explanation for that blue, a scientific explanation based on the laws of light refraction; but I forgot all about that and thought if there are angels and if I ever should be one—a most unlikely supposition any way I look at it—that is the color I should choose for a robe. Then I did remember the theory and I thought how silly it is, really, even though it may be as true as the temperature shown on a thermometer, which was 22 degrees above zero that day. I began to laugh at those "laws" we cite when we try to explain nature, because they aren't laws at all; they are nothing more than our own record of what happens in nature, monuments to man's own passion for words and figures.

"Holiday" means "holy day," of course. And "holy" is related to "whole" and even to "healthy." You have to go back to heathen times for those meanings, but there they are. Then I thought how readily the "holy" was tacked onto other words, indicating that in the old days there was reverence for a good many things we have now down-graded. There was holy mallow, for instance, a plebeian flower that we now grow in our dooryards and call the "hollyhock." There was a holy tree, with thorny leaves and red berries; we still call it "holy," but unknowingly, because we add another "l" and pronounce it "holly." There was even a fish called "holi butte," or holy flounder. We call it "halibut" and, if we like fish, we eat it any day in the week.

The point is that there were many holy things, even in everyday life, before man became so modern and so blasé, simply because man in the old days didn't think he knew all the answers. He could admit that even a tree or a fish was holy because it had a mystic, or at least a mysterious, air or quality. There was a touch of humility in man, who honestly admitted that he didn't create the earth or set the stars in their courses.

I looked at those big, firm parsnips, properly sweetened by the frost, and I wondered why a parsnip is better eating after it is frozen and why a potato isn't worth peeling after it has been nipped. I suppose a digital computer could come up with some kind of answer, if someone knew how to state the question for it; but we should take some things on faith, and I have faith in a parsnip. A tame parsnip. Certain wild parsnips are poisonous, as Socrates proved, I understand. The Greeks called the plant "hemlock," but it was a wild parsnip, and its essence put an end to Socrates' embarrassing questions. If they had had a machine to answer questions, the Un-Athenian Activities Committee probably would have indicted him for perjury instead of plain, everyday heresy.

I took a few parsnips into the house and went off to the woods beyond the pasture to mark a few trees as possibilities for Christmas, and to see how the partridges were doing. The birds were doing all right. I flushed three of them out of the two old, gnarled apple trees up there at the edge of a field that hasn't been farmed in fifty years, not since they quit using oxen around here, because tractors can't get up there. The partridges had been eating dormant apple buds. They get their Winter vitamins that way, even though a partridge doesn't know a vitamin from a verb. Something tells a partridge that an apple bud, or a birch or elm bud, is good to eat and will satisfy some seasonal hunger; and I don't care how many -ologists say it is a matter of instinct, because even they can't tell me what lies back of an instinct. Something does, something I can't see or compute or understand. I seriously doubt that it is an anthropomorphic god, but I have no doubt at all that it is something, or someone, that belongs to the tribe of gods who live in the remote places of this earth. This may make me a heathen; but, believe me, a devout heathen. I wish many times that I was as close to those gods as a partridge is.

I found the trees, and I marked them, and one of them will be down here at the house, come Christmas week. That tree will be decorated and lighted and set in front of a window that fronts on the road. Heathen though I may be, or pagan or pantheist perhaps, I want the world to know that Christmas has meaning for me. And I want to tell myself again that Christmas is the season to think about enduring life and the rebirth of faith and the big mysteries and the comforting beliefs that man cannot live without.

But that will be for later. The tree and all the other greens will not be brought in until the solstice is at hand.

Unless a blizzard intervenes, and it seldom does, we go up the mountain to gather greens the day before the solstice. It's an old custom with us, and it is rooted far back in the history of life on the land. You can't live with wind and weather, crops and the seasons, without knowing that the earth and the elements are fundamental matters with which it would be well to make peace from time to time. Besides, the Winter solstice is a time of diurnal crisis about which something should be done. Daylight has diminished to a point where, unless the sun turns back and climbs the sky again, night will engulf the world. The ancients knew this and, not being inhibited by the scientific illusion of human omnipotence, besought the sun itself to turn back, restore the daylight and ensure another Spring and Summer. They gathered evergreen boughs, symbolic of enduring life, and used them in their solstice ceremonies.

So, being somewhat skeptical of human omnipotence myself, I go out and gather the greens and bright Winter berries the day before the solstice. Nominally they are for decoration at the observance of the Nativity; but I recall that the early churchmen were not above adapting pagan holy days to their own purposes, and that even some churchmen of today can flex their faith on occasion. So I have a degree of precedence on my side. We put up the greens, the solstice passes safely, and by Christmas Day I can, if I wish, measure shadows and say a prayer of thanks in good conscience all around. My faith is renewed. Even the universe is in order. The year has survived its annual crisis, and who knows but my own small part in the venerable rites has been of some help?

We were discussing such matters at a small party the other evening and one man asked, "What is so important about a solstice? All it proves is that the earth spins on a tilted axis and moves in an elliptical orbit."

He was right, but only up to a point. He was indulging in oversimplification, thinking that if you state something in technical terms you have answered all questions about it. Few things are that simple. It is somewhat like defining man as a bipedal animal consisting of so many quarts of brine and so many pounds of chemical salts. That, too, is true—up to a point. But it omits, among other important elements, the thoughts, the dreams, the hopes, the fears, the fragile sense of morality, the love and the hate, and the sense of truth that make a man what he is.

Actually, the Winter solstice is an annual test of faith. Spring is the time of burgeoning growth, the urgency of life made manifest. Summer is a time of green abundance. Autumn is ripeness and harvest, bounty and completion. Faith is easy and belief is simple in a warm, green world. But man can face winter only with the security of unshaken certainty. Certainty of something fundamental, even so simple a matter as daylight and darkness. Cold deepens, daylight lessens, nights lengthen; and then the solstice occurs and provides the certainty of orderly, cycling change and great, enduring rhythms.

The more we seek, the clearer it becomes that there are no new securities, but only the old ones rediscovered. The solstice is a time of such rediscovery, for though I may define security in a dozen different ways the ultimate definition leads to the inner man and his relation to the earth and the universe. There must lie the certainty that gives life its meaning, just as there lies doubt, the lonely depth of cold and darkness. When I see the turn of the year I am reminded once again that faith and belief are neither foolish nor futile. That in itself is enough to make life worth living.

I suppose every countryman has been asked, time and again, why he persists in living where he does, apart from the crowd. And those of us who live in rural areas of harsh Winters sometimes ask ourselves about the necessity of fighting such a climate. The answers, when honestly given, are closely interwoven. A man needs roots. He needs to know the dimensions of a day and a year beyond the arbitrary statements of a clock and a calendar. He needs to know the integrity of a seed, of a growing woodland or cornfield or even of a tomato plant. He needs the truth of a star, and of flowing water, and of a hillside in the Spring of the year. And some of us need the four seasons, Winter as well as Summer, as proof that change is inevitable and eternal; as proof that life, like the year itself, is a continuity that demands participation. All of us need a sense of belonging, of being more than integers on a census chart.

This is a pretty lonely world, after all, despite the computations of the census takers and the neo-Malthusians. Man has worked himself so far out on the limb of rationality that there aren't many mysteries left except the really big ones such as where man came from and why, and what he is really doing here. He has banished so many comfortable mysteries that now he does not have much company except his own kind. And most men, if they would only admit it, are as baffled as I am by all these brand-new answers. The answers are glib answers, but not many of us have taken the time to appraise them. We have been too busy reading the figures off the dials and too busy jotting them down.

So here we are, trying our damnedest to make the world over in the image of our matter-of-fact data books, just as though we were omniscient gods with a sensible master plan. But we have no master plan, really. We are children in a great big sand box, seldom looking up at that spread of blue sky and that infinitude of stars to wonder what they mean. Or even to wonder what or who we are, playing here with our sand castles. All right, so we are protoplasm. What is protoplasm? And let's not get lost, this time, in the chemical formula for nucleic acid. What are we?

But let's get back to December and the holidays, which are a link to the past, whether we admit it or not. Holidays are for remembrance, if they have any meaning at all. We may not all remember the same things, and what we remember may not jibe with verifiable fact, but memory is a kind of root system for the human race, and without roots we are all damned to desolation.

As an instance, one keeper of the local memories told me a story about Ethan Allen. Ethan, he said, was a cold-weather boy who loved New England's rugged Winters. Winter was his playtime, and the whole holiday season, Thanksgiving through Twelfth Night, called for special celebration. I must add that Ethan Allen created quite a few legends around here before he recruited a crowd of Connecticut bully-boys at the local iron foundries of that day and went off to fight for freedom in the New Hampshire Grants. Anyway, according to this story, in the Fall of 1769 he recruited his rough-and-ready army but delayed his departure for the Grants till the day after Thanksgiving just so he could celebrate at a favorite local tavern. "Ethan." my storyteller said, "began by leading his men in prayer, since he was a very religious man. Then the boys began to have their fun." Before the fun was over, it seems, they almost tore the tavern apart. And my keeper of the legends added with a chuckle, "Good thing they left when they did. If they'd stayed for Christmas they'd likely have torn down Canaan Mountain."

Well, there was a link with the past, a fine, colorful link. I could accept it, not as historical truth, but as human truth. I did not bother to remind the reminiscent old gentleman that there wasn't any national Thanksgiving till well after 1769 or that Christmas wasn't exactly a secular celebration at that time. I did not even suggest that Ethan Allen, who fully expected to be reincarnated as a big white horse, wasn't much of a man for prayer. If the Ethan Allen of legend loved holidays and celebrated them in his own exuberant way, so be it, even if we have to invent a holiday or two to match the legend. I would even accept it if the legends said that Ethan hung one of his big woolen socks at the fireplace on Chirstmas Eve and found it filled with marzipan and gumdrops the next morning, with a fat Valencia orange in the toe. There is no rule that I know of which demands literal truth in the legends. It is the wonder that counts, the reach beyond prosaic facts, just as the holidays should mark the memory of reverence for matters beyond our ken but not beyond our aspiration.

In the Bible's Book of Joel it was said, "Your old men shall dream dreams, and your young men shall see visions," which probably was a venerable aphorism when it was first written down. It is still true. When all is said and done, we have little worth the having except the fruit of young men's visions and the substance of old men's dreams. The visions are the reach, the hope, and the dreams are the holding on, the anchor in the past. We need them both. The trouble comes when we renounce either of them, deny our birthright, or refuse to recognize our hopes. Without a yesterday there can be no tomorrow, and without both a yesterday and a tomorrow, today loses all meaning. Time is of a piece, not separable into isolated and unrelated bits. If the holidays had no meaning beyond their reminder of the past, of the once-exalted human purpose and a dream of peace and justice, they would still be an essential element in our fundamental ethic. The whole Christmas season is dedicated to one of the great events in the

Judeo-Christian tradition that is at the heart of our Western way of life.

So the day before the solstice we shall bring in one of the trees I have marked, and armloads of boughs and other greens, abiding by tradition. I almost said "guided by the same instinct that guides a partridge," and perhaps I should have. That, of course, would be primitive animism, of a kind. So call it tradition. We shall abide by tradition, in which the symbolism is written large. The tree is green with enduring life. The star at its tip is the star of Bethlehem; or, if one would rather, of the heavens at large. The lights—well: "And God said, 'Let there be light.'" And there are the fragile angels of shimmering foil and spun glass. There are the toy birds, because birds sang such joyous songs of celebration at the Birth. There is the tinsel, which glitters with the shimmer of faith. There is the artificial snow, white as real snow, white as the innocence of childhood.

We shall set out the candles on the window sills, going no further back than Shakespeare for meaning: "So shines a good deed in a naughty world." And hang the wreaths, which in their circularity signify continuity. In our house there is a pottery figure of Santa Claus holding a lighted candle aloft which will be there on the library table. Santa Claus, whom we remember with more than greedy sentiment, since his prototype was a saint, Saint Nicholas of Myra, fourth-century bishop of Asia Minor, patron of children, of schoolboys, of young men, and of sailors.

The symbols and the traditions. The miracle is that all over this land and much of the world there will be such symbols all through the holiday season. My own corner of New England is but one small patch, a pinpoint, in this vast sea of remembering, of old hope and persistent belief made manifest.

Winter and the Holiness

Somehow, I can't think of December without the holidays. They are not the whole of the month, but they bring it to a humanly meaningful focus, just as the solstice brings the natural year to a point of crisis and solution. We need Decembers in our lives.

Yesterday I was up on the mountain cutting pasture cedars, as we call them, for fence posts. We won't be using those posts till April, but this is a slack time, so to speak, and a man can't just sit. So Albert and I cut cedar posts, which are a kind of Winter harvest.

There were several inches of snow on the ground and the two brooks we had to cross to reach the cedars were mere threads of black water between shelves of white ice. But the Christmas ferns held proud, green fronds up to the sun and beneath the naked oaks were mats of running pine and ground cedar and the pines and hemlocks seemed to huddle in their groves. It was a brillant day with a dazzling sun far off in the southern reaches of the sky, but despite the sun our breath formed little clouds of frost crystals around our heads.

We set to work in what seemed a silent and deserted woodland, but before we had felled two cedars a crow flew over, black as sin and cawing loudly; then another, and another. Blue jays heard the crows and came to perch in the leafless maples, pompous as fat aldermen, and criticise our work. Then chickadees came, curious as cats, friendly as children, to twitter and peer and investigate each tree as we felled it.

We felled and trimmed and paused for a breather and to light our pipes. I looked out across the valley and thought that if we didn't already have December we would have to invent it, just so a man could come up there and see that the world is wider than a cornfield or a city block, that the sky is higher than a silo or skyscraper.

We worked till midafternoon, when the sun was down close to the horizon and a gray overcast began to spread up from the south. Then we shouldered our axes and went down the slope into the shadows of swiftly gathering dusk. Before we reached the far edge of the home pasture it began to snow, big, puffy flakes that nudged each other with a swishing sound like a whisper in the silence.

It was still snowing half an hour later when I went out to bring an armload of fireplace wood from the woodshed, but the temperature had dropped almost 10 degrees and the snow had been reduced to pellets that hissed in the wind that came whistling around the corner of the house. I looked to the north and knew that the Pole Star was there, fixed, beyond the cloud cover and that the Big Dipper lay close to the horizon, though I could not see it, pointing the time of all time as it has been since there were stars patterned in the sky. I looked out across the home pasture, a blur in the darkness, and knew the stark ridge was there, a ridge that was old when mankind was young. I knew these things, took both stars and mountain on faith. And I knew that I was one with the wind and the stars and the earth itself. December was all around me, simple as the glittering breath from my lungs, complex as the snowflake, and I was a part of the mystery, the wonder, and the awe. I was aware of the wholeness and the holiness of life, the reason beyond all my reasoning.

9

SNOWFALL AND FIRELIGHT

A group of us were sitting around the fire the other evening talking about such vital topics as the weather, local politics, taxes, and human cussedness. Eventually the conversation got around to the holidays we had capped with New Year's only a week before. The man in a plaid wool shirt said, "If we had more holidays there would be fewer tensions. You can't celebrate a holiday and start trouble at the same time."

"What we really need," said the man with a bow tie, "are longer Winters. Man is a comfort-loving animal who prefers to do his hell-raising in his shirt sleeves. Who ever picked a fight wearing galoshes and an overcoat?"

"We need both holidays *and* Winter," said the pipe-smoker, standing with his back to the fire. "Winter shows a man how insignificant he really is in the face of the elements. And holidays such as Christmas are a good excuse to be kind to your neighbors and tell each other how grateful you are for survival before you are really put to the test."

Two of the women murmured dissent. One of them said, "You are ignoring the religious significance of Christmas."

The pipe-smoker shook his head. "No. I am being realistic.

As realistic as the church. I don't recall many holy days, Winter or Summer, that interfere with planting or the harvest. The church says a man cannot live by bread alone, but it doesn't overlook the fact that without bread for the body you eventually run out of souls."

Nobody wanted to argue that point, since the pipe-smoker is treasurer of one of the local churches. The conversation turned to Christmas itself and the way we had observed it. Finally one of the women said, "Every year I swear I'm going to simplify things, and every year I don't. Why can't we get back to the real meaning of Christmas, the way it was in the beginning?"

The pipe-smoker turned to her and said blandly, "What was it like, that first Christmas?"

"It wasn't the rat race it is today," the woman said testily. "It was simple, and important. It was peace on earth, good will toward men. That's what it was."

The pipe-smoker nodded. "Sung by the heavenly host, and quoted from the Book of Luke. But even the shepherds had their doubts, and the innkeeper didn't subscribe to it at all. Not many people did. As I recall, King Herod soon sent out his hired assassins looking for the Child Jesus, and the doctrines that Jesus eventually preached weren't widely popular even with his own people. No, let's not go back to the beginning. Times are difficult enough now, with millions of people nominally subscribing to the ideal that Luke's heavenly host proclaimed in what was really a very hostile world."

Maybe the fact that we didn't get into a rousing argument at that point proves that human truculence is a warm-weather indulgence. But I am inclined to think it was more because when a few friends gather around the hearth on a brittle Winter night the trend is toward the warmth of understanding rather than the heat of contention. Somehow, the fagots of the fanatic don't burn very brightly in a fireplace.

Maybe the fact that we had all been shoveling snow or forking hay or cutting firewood had something to do with it too. You don't often come in from such everyday Winter chores burning with indignation and full of the urge to right all the world's wrongs and correct all the absurdities before bedtime. Maybe you should, but you don't.

Most of us, even here in the country, know that the state of the world is something less than perfect. We also know that it has been that way for a long time and that man seems to have a genius for making a periodic mess of his own affairs. But for a few months each year we see the natural world quiet down and mask its own shortcomings and man's most obvious failures under a clean white blanket that, superficially at least, invites a brand-new chapter to be written. And man has so contrived his calendar that Winter itself provides a new start, a new year in which all things are theoretically possible. That in itself is sufficient reason for a holiday season. The religious significance merely reinforces the natural reasons, gives them spiritual meaning and importance.

Not long ago I was asked why the countryman is, as the questioner put it, "so damned optimistic." I said, "You should talk to some of my neighbors. Year after year they are on the verge of bankruptcy and starvation, to hear them tell it. But they keep right on going, one way and another."

"That's exactly what I mean," my questioner said. "They don't face facts."

And I had to point out that that is exactly what they do. They face facts every day of their lives. Every countryman does. Such facts as the weather and the seasons, growth and harvest, cause an effect. You can't live close to the land and fail to believe in the basic fact of life, even in some probable purpose for life. That may be the enduring reason for the country, to perpetuate such belief against the recurring times when doubt and despair threaten to take over. Somehow, it is difficult to subscribe to the inevitability of disaster when you are confronted, year after year, by the evidence of a natural world which so obviously persists and even succeeds in its own purposes in the face of all kinds of hazards. Those aren't the facts my questioner had in mind, but they have outlasted most of the "facts" based on man's own circumstance.

Man likes to think he is the boss here, and life might be much simpler if he really were, though that is debatable. Anyway, he isn't the ultimate boss, and every day of my life I see the evidence. Man is not much more than a tenant here, and he has survived and evolved biologically in large part by chance. Chance and his own wit and good fortune. As a countryman I know that dispassionate nature, which is quite unaware of my existence except as a devilishly ingenious predator, will dispossess me unless I keep constantly at work maintaining my temporary suzerainty. Unless somebody picks up my axe and my brush hook the day after I am gone, these acres will start reverting to brush and timber before my grave is green. Every countryman faces such facts, whether he talks about them or not. He lives by them.

I doubt that one can be either optimistic or pessimistic if he lives with the land and the seasons. Basically, one is forced into acknowledgment of fundamental certainties—the certainty of life and death and eternal change. There is little you can do about last year except remember it, and you have to face next year as it comes. I have yet to meet the man who can hurry the departure of a New England Winter or divert the path of a Midwestern blizzard. But I have no doubt that this winter will eventually end, as all Winters have, and that we will be able to plow and plant out fields again and, in due time, gather their harvest. And I know from experience that nobody can either hurry or delay a harvest. If life close to the land teaches nothing else, it does enforce the lesson of patience.

I was reading a history of the American Revolution the other night and was struck by the author's emphasis on the number of "desertions" from the ranks of the Continental Army. That city-bred author seemed to forget that at the time of the Revolution close to 95 per cent of the population of the colonies was rural. Most of the soldier-farmers were farmers first and soldiers second, countrymen who knew that a battle might be postponed but that the growing season couldn't be. They went home to do the chores between engagements at arms. And after the chores were done most of them went back to the fighting.

Wars are not fought that way any more, not in "civilized" countries, at least. But the countryman of today, faced with Winter's demands, can understand what happened, and why. If his attention wavers a bit from today's budget of news about crisis and disaster, it may be because his heating system is having a tantrum, the water pipes have frozen, and there's a leak in the roof. Such things have to be handled, here and now. Life has to go on. Besides, time after time he has seen how today's crisis shrinks to next week's footnote to a newly headlined disaster.

Perils, after all, are not new to mankind. They come today in large, economy-size packages that cost far more than we can afford and they have a louder crackle-snap-pop than they ever had before. But the early Greeks had words for both "peril" and "crisis," roots of the words we use today. And, whether he had words for them or not, the first man who took shelter in a cave was not entirely free from threat and danger. If he had been he wouldn't have retreated to a hole in the rocks.

Last Fall, when we still had shirt-sleeve weather, a fervid man full of tensions came up here into the hills for a weekend and his host asked a few of us over to meet him. As the talk developed, it seemed that this man's mission was to warn everyone within hearing that the world was about to collapse around our ears and probably would bury us in the debris. We listened as politely as we could while he developed his theme, but finally one short-tempered countryman asked this fellow if he had ever read history.

"History," the man said firmly, "is one long chronicle of trouble. Anyone who reads it intelligently must know that it points directly at the crossroads where we stand today."

My fellow countryman suggested that maybe he had skipped a few pages here and there in his reading.

The man laughed. "Which pages?"

"The pages between the wars, when men stopped long enough to speculate on what life would be like if mankind weren't quite so cantankerous. The pages about philosophers and religious leaders and poets and artists. And, if I may say so, farmers."

"Why do you add farmers?" the man asked with a smile. "Farmers have always been the last to realize what was happening. The provinces, since the days of the early Roman Empire, have always been remote and smug in their ignorance."

"So you write them off," the countryman said, "just as the

Romans did. And who inherited the Roman Empire when it fell to pieces? The provincials, as you call them. That is why I added the farmers to my list."

"And what happened to civilization when the provincials took over?" the man demanded.

"It purged itself, and eventually it took on new life," the countryman said. And he added, "In those pages that you missed, my friend, is the story of civilization itself, which always has withered last and sprouted first close to the land. In the provinces."

There was more to it, a good deal more, but it came out at the end of the evening not far from that point of firm disagreement. The fervid man clearly thought that he had fallen, if not among thieves, at least among men blind to realities. And most of us provincials thought he was overstating the case for total disaster.

I must add that before we were snugged in for the Winter, a few weeks later, the crisis that nervous visitor was so sure would set off the holocaust had become only another footnote to current history and a new crisis had taken its place on the front pages.

That, as I said, was in shirt-sleeve weather. Right now, in galoshes and overcoats, or Winter boots and storm coats, we probably wouldn't give such a testy man that much of a challenge. We very likely would just let him talk himself out and get back to local politics and taxes and the weather.

I hope I haven't given the impression that I believe life on the land automatically makes a man wise, tolerant, and full of enlightened understanding. I believe nothing of the kind. A rural lunkhead is just as witless as his city cousin, and a bigot is a bigot wherever you meet him. Stupidity is an individual achievement, not a geographical consequence. But I do believe that prefabricated opinion is somewhat less common and mass emotions are less infectious when one lives somewhat apart from the crowds.

Obviously, the countryman now is a member of a minority group. But his minority status has a degree of flexibility. He can join the majority by simply moving off the land. He is not born into a caste system, nor is he set apart by his religious belief or the color of his skin. Countrymen come in all colors and with a whole spectrum of faiths and opinions. But except in certain blighted areas where they are trapped in the same way slum dwellers are trapped in the cities, most countrymen live where they do and as they do as a consequence of choice—they went there or they stay there because that is where, for a variety of reasons including sheer inertia, they prefer to live.

There is really nothing new in the shift of population from the country to the cities. Ancient Rome passed laws to restrict such migration from the provinces, though stout provincial youths were conscripted for the Roman armies and many a provincial lass bore natural sons for lusty Roman citizens. The growth of any commercial society lures the restless and the dispensable from the land in search of affluence or ease or excitement or the mere exhilaration of a new environment. We live in a foot-loose age, an age of shifting populations everywhere; and the machine that is not only its symbol but its dominant characteristic creates a paradox that still baffles us. It creates an insatiable demand for manpower for a time, then matures into progressive independence of the very men who created it, thus becoming a kind of modern Moloch calling for endless human sacrifice. There, in the machine, is today's social tragedy, not on the land.

Someday perhaps a brave social philosopher will turn his back on the fads and fashions in his "discipline," as the academic pontificators insist on calling any specialized area of thought, and examine work, plain everyday work, as a basic factor in human progress and culture and an essential element in that elusive satisfaction we call happiness. If anyone were inclined to undertake such an unlikely project, I might offer a few notes with which to start.

Ideally, man should be able to live on this fruitful earth with a minimum of labor, but he early became discontented with life in a cave and a diet of fruit and nuts. Every change he made, however, demanded work—to build a shelter, to plant a crop, to protect first a family, then a tribe.

Every society that man has organized was based on the labor of someone. Even the idealists and Utopians never found a way to do away with work; the best they could do was to apportion and minimize it. And the most successful of their dream societies were based on community labor, each to his own skills, and exaltation of work well done. Less idealistic societies have tried to escape work by enslaving their neighbors, domesticating draft animals, or building machines. And always there have been those who lived by their wits, and always at the expense of others who had to do the work.

With almost cyclic inevitability, cultures that were based on individual freedom from work became decadent, cynical, and weak rather than vital and happy and strong. The work-is-a-curse myth led to war and ultimate disaster, and the provincials who had never succeeded in doing away with work inherited the remnants of a culture based on leisure. Man, being what he is, had to start the cycle all over again.

But down at the base of all cultures was the land and those who lived upon it. There was where the food was produced, and the raw materials for commerce and industry. Whether he subscribed to the myth or not, the man on the land could provide a large degree of comfort and security, if not a real Garden of Eden, if he was willing to work at it. And work he did. He even had his satisfactions in accomplishment. If there was a workless hereafter, that would be a bonus that he had earned and probably would appreciate. For a time. He knew, from experience, that he would be bored and restless after a few heavenly years. He would begin to look for March and April, the passing of Winter and the coming of Spring when the land needed his attention. He probably would even remember June and haying season, when a man worked a sweaty sixteen hours a day and gloried in his own strength, though he did appreciate night and a chance to rest and sleep.

That isn't the whole story, by any means. It isn't even a good start, though it might be a take-off point. The fact is that every civilization has been at its strongest, in human terms at least, when it was in some stage of the pioneering phase; when man was out there building a civilized society at the near edge of a wilderness, dreaming not of a sweatless utopia but of accomplishment with his own thew and muscle. Without that foundation there is neither commerce nor industry, neither art not philosophy. Both civilization and culture must be rooted somewhere, and all roots grow best in the soil itself.

But this is no season to be argumentative about these or any other matters. It's still Winter up in these hills, and we are still a bit influenced by the holidays, when we were kind to our neighbors and grateful for survival, as we always are at this time of year. Grateful also, I must add, for Winter's relative leisure. Relative, understand, not complete. Most of us are out every day shoveling snow or forking hay or cutting wood or tending the livestock. But some of us stop from time to time in the midst of such laborious chores to look at the world. I did, only a little while ago, and I wished that tense, hurrying, crowded people all over the world could see it under this clean white blanket, just waiting for a new chapter to be written. A chapter that would revise some of the old myths about work and happiness and the desirability of an eternal holiday hereafter.

10

MORALITY AND A NOD TO ETHICS

February was inserted in the calendar in an effort to correct human errors in counting up to twelve. Or maybe it was thirteen, since February originally marked the shift from a lunar calendar to one based on the sun, and there are more than twelve but less than thirteen lunar months in any solar year. In any case, I find February tolerable, if not exactly reassuring, for that reason. It shows that man, however much he fumbles, does reach for accuracy even when his counting leads him beyond the range of the fingers on his two hands. There are times, as when buying eggs or calculating interest, when one should know the difference between twelve and thirteen.

February was named for a feast of purification, which occurred about midmonth. This is doubly significant. In the area where I live, February certainly purifies a man. It makes him willing to confess sins, errors, and shortcomings for which he may be only slightly to blame, in hopes of coming safely through to March and, eventually, to Spring. And, in a moral sense, any time dedicated to purification and reform deserves approval and a degree of applause. Repentance, even without remorse, comes more easily while the weather is still making a man aware of human frailty. By June he is flexing his muscles and bragging about his hay crop or his gross production of pig iron as though he, personally, made the grass grow or laid down the ore beds.

Perhaps that is why, in February, we are briefly tempted to believe those legislators, both state and national, who so often choose this time for annual debate about their ethics. It starts with a revelation of wrongdoing in high places. It progresses to a discussion of the nature and extent of the wrongdoing. Then it gets to the point of argument, not about ethics, but about legal right and legal wrong. The idea seems to be that if the law doesn't specifically forbid wrongdoing, then it isn't wrong, but that maybe there should be another law. Or, as they put it, a code of ethics. And that is where the seeds of skepticism begin to sprout in those of us who grew up with the idea that conscience and individual responsibility, not statute law, are at the heart of morality and ethics. By the time they have talked themselves out, drawn up a "code," amended it to a point of casuistry, and then decided that passage of any code at all would be a slap at their own integrity, we know that it was all a matter of ritual, a part of the age-old purification ceremony. Even the sacrificial lamb is usually spared, with only a token singe.

Once in a while the matter of ethics is brought briefly into focus by others than the legislators, as when Earl Warren, Chief Justice of the United States Supreme Court, made the public suggestion that we needed men trained in a new profession, men he called "counselors of ethics." Such counselors, the Chief Justice said, "might prove helpful to the modern business man, politician, academic executive, and other professionals who wish to discern the right." In discussing his proposal he observed that "in civilized life, law floats in a sea of ethics," and he pointed out that without ethics, law itself could not exist.

There can be little dissent from such statements about law and ethics, particularly when made by the head of our highest court. But even a countryman with little legal knowledge or experience knows that there are shoals in that sea of ethics which neither lawyers nor jurists seem to have charted. And the whole idea of delegating this matter of ethics to a select group of counselors seems a strange way out. As I understand it, a defendant before the bar is considered legally insane if he is unable to distinguish right from wrong. Have we reached a point where we must declare our businessmen, politicians, academic executives, and other professionals legally insane? Are we now so deep in the morass of moral confusion that we must abandon the last vestige of conscience and delegate moral responsibility to an "ethical counselor"?

I had always thought that the sea of ethics in which the law floats consists of our traditions of truth and justice and integrity and the responsibility of the individual for his own actions. Ethics, of course, is a philosophical concept, but it usually is defined as a system of moral principles. And "moral" is commonly accepted as meaning the quality of actions and attitudes that result from a man's natural or inherited sense or reasoned judgment of what is right and proper. Thus it all seems to boil down to a matter of accepted traditions of individual actions and social necessity. Take away individual responsibility, delegate morality to a group of specialists, and that sea of ethics shrinks to the dimensions of a very small and very shallow pond.

The heart of any system of ethics in what we think of as

civilized society is the accountability of the individual for his own actions. And since the legal system we have evolved also holds the individual accountable for what he does, our law truly floats in that sea of ethics. But law is essentially a means of regulating individual conduct for the safety and security of society, and ethics is a matter of personal conduct based on traditional standards of morality, of fundamental right and wrong, without respect to society at large. Ethics and law are not always or necessarily dedicated to the same end, and legal justice is not always or necessarily moral or ethical justice.

To put ethics on the same plane as law, as the legislators tend to do in their annual purgation of the conscience, seems to be another step in the retreat from individual responsibility. And the "ethical counselor" suggestion of Chief Justice Warren is an even further step in that direction. As life has become more complex, we have delegated more and more responsibility for our own actions. We tend to leave religion to the churches, prayer to the preachers. We blame our parents for our frustrations and failures. We ask the psychiatrists to solve our emotional problems. We dump our conjugal dilemmas on marriage counselors and divorce courts. We leave it to the schools to teach standards of conduct and morality to our children.

If our educators, too, now need the guidance of special counselors to distinguish right from wrong, where are we going to turn for those counselors?

Perhaps the legislators are closer to the solution than the Chief Justice, after all. Their homilies and their lip service to ethics and morality are at least reminders that somewhere in the race conscience there are vestiges of ethical standards. And their reluctance to make more than token gestures toward codifying ethics on the statute books implies, whether they know it or not, that morality is essentially a personal matter and that laws are sorry substitutes for conscience.

I sometimes wonder if we couldn't dispense with those pious debates about ethical codes, and with any need for professional counselors of ethics as well, if we restored February to its old status as a time of personal purification. I wouldn't advocate making it a month of public breast-beating with *"Mea culpa"* as its theme song. We have enough of that now, and too little of it has the ring of sincerity. Nor would I make it an official month of prayer and meditation, no matter how dedicated the preachers and even the elders of the churches may be. Evangelists tend to explicate their chosen doctrines, and theology is not necessarily the same as ethical morality.

What I have in mind is the kind of self-examination a man can do in private, at least in the privacy of his own mind when he is in the mood to listen to his conscience. A whole month of that might be too much for most of us. But February, after all, is the shortest month, and February days average only about ten and a half hours of daylight. The nights are long, but even a conscience has to sleep sometime. Troubled dreams might be a problem, but we all have them, don't we? We have our own ways of coping with them.

Maybe my thinking is somewhat colored by what an old countrywoman said a year ago when I went to see how she fared during a three-day February storm. She lives alone and I had to wallow through four-foot drifts to reach her door. She took her own time about letting me in, but I found her safe and well though in no mood for entertaining visitors.

"You interrupted my February thinking," she said sharply, making me feel like a naughty boy as the snow from my boots melted into a puddle on her living room rug.

I said I was sorry and suggested that her neighbors were worried about her welfare.

"You needn't have been," she said. "If I need help I'll let somebody know." Then she said, "A body needs some time and privacy to think. All Summer long I'm busy doing, and folks are coming and going till after Christmas. Then it takes awhile to get acquainted with myself again before we get a good thinking-storm, like this one. I was in the middle of counting when you came banging at the door."

"Counting what?" I asked.

"Counting up the good and the bad, to see if I deserved to live another year," she said tartly.

"Of course you do," I said. "Everybody knows——"

"That's for me to say," she interrupted, "when I've finished counting. You made me lose track and now I've got to start all over again. Shut the door tight when you go out. Good-bye!"

It could be, of course, that the perennial ethics debaters are doing their February thinking too. But they do it so publicly, and they are so sententious. And they count up the good and the bad for others, not for themselves. They talk about laws instead of conscience. They want to pass the buck to the courts.

You really can't pass the buck without renouncing man's unique endowment and inheritance—his capacity for thought and reason and his awareness of truth and virtue. That is where conscience dwells, in the deep-down knowledge that there is a difference between right and wrong, truth and falsehood, duty and dereliction. Possession of that knowledge is one of the fundamental differences between man and the other animals.

Sentimentalists sometimes point to pseudo-ethics among the birds and animals—protection and training of the young, respect for territorial rights, the fact that only the rare rogue among predators kills for the mere killing. And the cynics sometimes say that man's ethics are expedient rather than intrinsic, pointing to murder, theft, promiscuity, and sadism as expressions of man's natural impulses.

Both the sentimentalist and the cynic are wrong. Animals are essentially creatures of instinct and impulse, and man has the innate concept of morality to curb his impulses and instincts. Whatever curbs there may be to animal reactions, especially when they seem to conform to human standards of exemplary behavior, are dictated by the instinct for survival, individually and as a species. There is no evidence of what we call conscience in them.

The nearest approach to ethics, as we use that term, probably is among the social insects. But even there the parallels are deceptive. A colony of bees or ants does have its rigid code of conduct, and every member of the colony appears to be bound by it. But it is a code imposed by instinct and enforced by habit, not by processes of thinking or the dictates of conscience. The whole colony is organized on a system of castes and assigned duties, with no need for thought nor noticeable capacity for it. Conceivably, failure to abide by caste and duty might be wrong; but there is no room, or even excuse, for debate about such matters in an ant's life. The sole purpose of the colony is survival. The individual cannot change its status. For the achievement of a system of ethics there must be a matter of choice. Without choice there is neither good nor bad, but only what is. There is no morality in a life of complete and inflexible routine.

Yet in nature as a whole there is a recognizable degree of morality, even in the human sense. Fundamentally, it is the enforcement of the basic law of cause and effect. Within the limits of that law there is some measure of choice and action, but always with the certainty of effect as a consequence of cause. What we call the balance of nature arises from that law, though the term itself is deceiving because the balance is forever shifting. But virtually all the conditions of life as we know it are dependent on cause and effect.

Crowd any environment with too many members of the same species, plant, animal, bird, or insect, and the conditions become hostile to that species. Overcrowding tends to kill, by starvation or disease.

Alter any environment radically and you make it intolerable for its existing forms of life. In the face of an advancing ice sheet, or encroaching waters, or enduring drouth, all but the most hardy forms of bird, animal, and insect life must move. Plant life, unable to move, is destroyed.

Poison or pollute the air, the water, or the soil and you kill the customary life of that environment or accelerate adaptation by a few species that have or quickly can develop a degree of tolerance for the new conditions. Widespread use of persistent organic pesticides has killed birds, animals, and benevolent insects as well as the unwanted pests, and has forced evolution of resistent weed plants, virulent germs, and hostile insects.

Strew the atmosphere with atomic dust, ionized particles, and other unpredictable debris and you alter the conditions of weather sources in ways still only vaguely understood. No matter where we live, here on earth, we have to live with the weather and its consequences. Even in the modern city's zones of artificial weather, we are at the mercy of the natural weather elsewhere which largely controls the supply of our food crops and our potable water.

Such broad examples of cause and effect are as enduring as the earth itself. But until man evolved, with his capacity for thought, memory, and understanding, cause and effect were in the nature of blind, inflexible forces of which no form of life was more than instinctively aware.

Very early in his race history, however, man must have become consciously aware of cause and effect and known that there were consequences, even personal consequences, to his actions. From such awareness must have come the first vague sense of right and wrong, if only in terms of survival. A comparative physical weakling endowed with few effective natural weapons, man survived only because of his superior intelligence, his knowledge that he could not avoid the consequences of his own actions. From such knowledge must have grown a sense of responsibility and obligation, which are at the root of a moral sense.

Thus he progressed beyond the stage at which the social insects, for instance, appear to have stopped, the point where survival was the sole purpose of life. He became an individual aware of himself and of his capacity to choose among several possible courses of action. He was becoming a thinking, remembering, understanding man.

Living close to the land, in many ways a part of the land, he learned that there were matters of personal responsibility that were difficult, if indeed at all possible, to delegate. He evolved various pantheons, with gods of all degree, to whom he could delegate most decisions, but in so doing he made himself responsible to those gods and accountable to them. One way and another, he established standards of conduct for himself, built ethical systems for his own guidance. He acknowledged cause and effect in his own life and actions and he found it profitable, for his conduct as well as his conscience, to count up the good and the bad in his own life. He found it possible to face the truth of himself.

More and more, as we have quit the land and the everyday evidence of that basic law of cause and effect, we have tended to forget and ignore the fundamentals of that "sea of ethics" in which our modern law floats. We have moved more and more toward the excuse of the law itself, not realizing that without the sea of ethics the law goes aground on what may prove to be a barren and rocky shore. Bit by bit, we edge toward the moral desert where the social insects isolated themselves eons ago, a place of instinct but with no fertile soil in which choice and decision can grow and live.

It is not a happy prospect, though perhaps it is easier to contemplate in February, say, than in July or August, when the ants and the bees are out of the egg and pupa and active everywhere. Now the countryman at least is aware of the great rhythm of the seasons and the inflexible rule of change. He may be a fallible creature, a talkative, argumentative dealer in moral nonsense and ethical chicanery, but he is a man, not an ant.

Being man, he is aware of man's predicament, if not of man's estate. And the season does tend to purify a man, one way or another; at least, it helps to clarify his thinking and demand a degree of scope in his speculations. There isn't much a man can do about a February storm except last it out and ponder his state of being. If he has been foresighted, he can endure it and come safely through to Spring. But he can't lie about it, even to himself. He can't steal from April to ameliorate February. He can't burn fuel that he promised to cut, but didn't, last November, nor can he feed his cattle hay that he failed to cut last June. Whatever his shortcomings, they begin to catch up with him by now.

The other evening, after I had spent an hour reading the text of the latest debate about ethics and legality, I went out and looked at the night. The stars of infinity were all about me, filling the sky. The hills of eternity were stark in the snow glow that relieved the darkness. There was a vastness and a timelessness that made man and all his works seem of minor consequence and brief duration. The only thing of importance even to my egocentric awareness was the fact that I, one of a unique species, was here to see and wonder at ultimate meanings. And I wondered why man, the biological upstart, should be endowed with an innate sense of right and wrong, truth and falsehood, while ants and bees and woodchucks and robins and trout seem to possess so little beyond the insistent impulse toward survival. Why man, so endowed with this precious knowledge, should persist in debating its very existence.

The night itself was unaware of me. I could not alter the course of the stars or raise a moon or whistle up the wind. I could not fashion a snowflake or unlock the river's ice. I could only stand there, aware of the night, and know the haunting sense of wonder, the enduring questions about man and the universe.

Perhaps the wonder and the questions are enough for a man to prove his membership in the race, on a February night. Perhaps there are no answers.

11

THE CERTAINTY OF CHANGE

It is best to live in a land of four seasons. I have to say this firmly every March because then come days when I would gladly forfeit the beauty of New England's May and the glory of our October just to be either warm or cold, wet or dry, the year around. March can try a man's soul. But it can also make him exult, on an occasional day; and then I wouldn't willingly give up one minute of it.

If I try to pin this down, find some logic in what is obviously an emotional response and a sensory reaction, the best I can do is say that March is essentially a promise, a satisfying process in the constant state of change. This isn't really definitive, of course, since time and life are constantly changing and every season, in that sense, is a kind of promise of something different tomorrow or next week. But if I go on and say that there is more satisfaction, and even excitement, in beginnings than there is in endings, I am at least approaching an explanation.

A January snowstorm has excitement and, in one sense, satisfaction. It is a seasonal achievement. But its excitement is based on the depth of the snow, the degree of the cold, the strength of the wind, and the duration of the storm. Such a storm is primarily a challenge, but not an enduring challenge. I know from experience that the wind will ease off, the cold will moderate, the storm will end, and eventually the snow will melt. Beyond the enduring mystery of the snowflake and the aching beauty of a snowdrift, such a storm leads to nothing more than renewal of the ground water in the country and costly inconvenience in the city.

A series of hot July days also has excitement, particularly when they build atmospheric tension that explodes into thunderstorms that shake the hills and roar through the woodlands. There is satisfaction in seeing how July heat inspires the corn to reach for the sky, in the spectacular proof on every hand of the urgency of growth and ripeness. But thunderstorms pass, the green leaf proceeds with its quiet miracle of photosynthesis, the blossom is fertilized and becomes a pod or a berry or a pome or an ear. Those who live with the land tend to look upon this with the satisfaction of personal accomplishment, but we know most of these things would happen even if we sat in the shade and didn't turn a hand. What happens in July was established in March.

And right there is the reason for the countryman's response, on one of those rare but perfect March days. It is as simple as the delight in new discovery of an idea. I make the distinction, new discovery, not new idea, because what is happening in March is as old as the changing seasons themselves. It is new only as we see it again, fresh and almost innocent. There it is, the whole span of tremendous possibilities, incredible potentials, discovered afresh on a fine March day.

If your senses are not wholly atrophied you can feel it in the air elsewhere than in the open country. But to understand it you must be in touch with the earth. Feeling and understanding are quite different processes. Walk the fields on such a day and, no matter how the wind may veer and the air shift, the subtle truth invades you through the very soles of your feet. It rectifies your pulse and becomes a part of the rhythm of your being. And that is where understanding dwells.

We had such a day last week. It came, as such days often do, in the wake of February's last storm, a visitation of sleet and snow that avoided three temptations to quit and two temptations to turn into a blizzard. It lasted almost three days, lapping over into the second day of March. But for all the huffing and puffing, it brought less than a foot of snow. It blew itself out at last, though the temperature hung in the low 20s for another twenty-four hours. Then change set in, first a rise in temperature, then a mild, dry wind. The snow turned to slush, then to water, and I had ponds in every hollow in my pastures. Brooks surged and the black water of the river was briefly white with huge shards of ice from the coves upstream. There was only a moderate amount of frost in the soil, thanks to a snow cover that came before Christmas and remained until this thaw, and that frost was soon melted. The pasture ponds sank into the soil overnight.

Then came that day, with a clear sky, a dazzling sun, and the temperature an even 60 by midmorning. I smelled it, even in the house. I had to go and see, sense, perhaps participate, so I put on a lightweight windbreaker and went outdoors.

I walked out across the home pasture where the grass was the color of dead oak leaves still clinging to the trees in the woodland. The sod was soggy underfoot. But that very brownness, that oozy sogginess, was meaningful. Beneath the dead grass stems were live roots already awakening to the moisture, and the soil itself was fecund with hidden seeds, a hundred kinds of seeds; and all those seeds were feeling the first faint persuasion of warm moisture. In them, waiting only for more warmth, more direct light from a sun still approaching the vernal equinox, were roots and stems and leaves and blossoms and, in those blossoms, the triumph of another seeding. Even in a grass seed, so much smaller than the proverbial mustard seed that also was there, waiting for the summons of the sun.

I crossed the pasture to the far margin, and there in the fence row were alder bushes and hazelnut brush and gray birch saplings. There were the dried stems of bee balm and mint and goldenrod, the prickly stems of barberry that grew from bird droppings and last Fall was full of scarlet berries that lured partridges down from the mountainside for a November feast.

At first glance the fence row brush was Winter-barren, but when I looked more closely I saw that the birches and the alders were hung with tiny catkins still tightly closed. I saw them a month ago, when the snow was knee-deep, for they are defiant of late Winter. But now they were subtly relaxed, not yet open but no longer tight as a clenched fist. They, like the seeds in the pasture soil, were waiting for more sun, more warmth and light. Then, at their proper time, when the inconspicuous female catkins were thrusting forth their receptive styles, they would begin to flex their scales and release their incredible wealth of pollen.

I went on, through the fence row and up the mountainside to the first ledge. There were still patches of snow in the hemlock thickets, but all the seep springs were trickling, little rivulets leaching the lingering frost from the thin topsoil. I stopped at a low-branched red oak and saw the buds in all the axils of the leaves that still clung, tight buds yet but holding within them the pattern of leaf and twig and blossom, even of the acorn, all compacted in a bud no larger than a grain of wheat.

There was green in the woods, but only the green that has been there all Winter—the evergreen fronds of Christmas fern, the trailing partridgeberry, the mats of ground pine and ground cedar, and the conifers, the pines and the hemlocks. March is not a green time. But—and this is the point—there was the feel, the sense, the elusive understanding, of greenness already determined. There was, upon the pastureland, in the fence row, and in the woodland, a commitment to a green tomorrow. It was even more than the certainty of change; it was both the pattern for that change and latitude within that pattern.

And that, to me, is a basic part of the excitement. If it were possible to say with certainty that beneath that particular red oak would grow three clumps of Chistmas fern, no more, no less, or that in the fence row one white pine seedling would appear and thrive beside the gate, the wonder and surprise would be gone. I do know, as surely as I know anything, that unless there is sudden and total change in the climate there will be no date palms growing in my woodland; but within the broad span of natural possibilities, almost anything else can happen. Seeds sprout, eggs hatch, plants grow, when and where they find hospitable conditions, and I can only partially and temporarily govern or alter those conditions.

There in the pasture and the woodland, that perfect March day, I was aware of beginnings. And, perhaps even more importantly, I was aware of endings only in terms of human projects. Almost nothing in nature adds up to completion. All the forms of life I know, including myself, are a result of change and are still changing. Not even the earth is or ever will be complete and stable. The mountain just beyond my home pasture is forever crumbling away, and the valley where I live is slowly being filled with silt. I shall never see the ultimate consequence, if there is an ultimate; but when I reach beyond my own limited experience with time, my own lifetime, I am inevitably aware of the endless processes of change.

But right now, today, in March, I need not reach beyond the span of the year to be aware of the deliberate potentialities all around me, the root, the seed, the bud, the invisible beginnings of another cycle in the great rhythms of life and time.

We cannot go back, any more than the root can return to the seed, the blossom to the bud, or the chick to the egg. The commitment has placed us where we are and barred the paths whence we came. But, being the creatures we are, endowed with memory and analytic reason, we can look back and reach for understanding. Looking back, we see that somewhere along the way we sold our birthright of wonder for a bowl of facts. We replaced the great simplicities which make life comprehensible with the complexity of our own lives. Jealous of the old gods, we created a pantheon of statistics and norms and averages and endowed them with omnipotence. We narrowed the horizons of understanding, then denied that we had done it and boasted about our new depths of knowledge.

Unable to account for the universe, we have counted the visible stars, named the galaxies, and analyzed the astral spectra. Unable to fathom time, we have dissected the day into hours, the hours into minutes, and finally achieved the microsecond. Baffled by life and unable to create so much as a fertile mustard seed, we have peered into the atom and discovered another universe. Unwilling to accept ourselves, we have invented neuroses, psychoses, compulsions, and aberrations to excuse our own confusion.

Too often we have mistaken facts for answers and data for truth. Fragmented ourselves by the socio-economic-industrial machine we have created, we accept fragmented answers from the machines, forgetting that even the most elaborate computer can only analyze, reduce a problem to its components, and fails utterly to reveal that mysterious combination and unique synthesis that gives man as well as the universe both form and meaning.

If there were some way to program the mystery of a March day and ask the computer for an answer, the reply would undoubtedly come out as data on temperature, humidity, wind velocity, and, possibly, sap pressure in a maple tree. And that, I insist, is no answer, but only a group of facts. If I am to understand even those facts, let alone speculate on their total meaning, I must be in touch with both the earth and the elements. House myself away from wind and weather, isolate myself from the source of life, which is the earth itself, and I have severed the roots of reality. I will have alienated myself from beginnings and surrounded myself with inevitable endings. Cities decay, machines rust away, facts and data become fossils in the sediment of the accumulating yesterdays. And the big, eternal questions remain: Who am I? Where am I? What time is it?

It would be so simple if we could go back, know again the wonder and the ease of acceptance, with the kind of understanding that only time and the generations ever evolve. But the nearest to such a return that I can manage is by losing myself in the annual miracle of the season's first stir of beginnings. I cannot really participate, though I am remotely a part of it, for mine is a going on, an existence, and a sentience that were determined for me long ago. But, being sentient, I can feel it and, to a degree, I can understand it. And insofar as I do understand, I know that life, the wholeness of life, is not only reality but inevitability. I am not an ant or a newt or a lizard, and I have no roots literally in the soil like an oak or an anemone, but I am of their kind and company. I partake of rhythms that dominate their lives. I am a member of the whole vast community of life, not merely of the community of my own kind.

Their beginnings are not my beginnings, except in the remote sense that we all are participants in a common source. Yet the stirrings and faint quickenings of a March day touch me, when I submit myself, and somewhere at my remote nerve ends they renew my own life. I am made a part of something bigger than myself, more enduring than the human crowd. I am subtly informed, by the humus underfoot and the tight bud on the twig, that the whole philosophy of endings is false. I have become a part of enduring forces, the great surge of life.

Nature does not simplify. Nature proliferates. Its whole purpose, so far as we can discern purpose, is infinite variety. It is man who would simplify, classify, and reduce to formulas and patterns; but the more he attempts, the less he achieves because he is surrounded by change and variation. No matter how thoroughly he may list and name and demarcate, the surge of change is always ahead of him. Nature does not even pause to teach, being neither oracle nor object lesson. If I would learn I must watch and listen, not hide myself away and surround myself with man-made endings and ephemeral human answers.

Every Autumn I am tempted to mistake ripeness for completion. The apple reddens, the ear matures on the cornstalk, the dry pod splits and spills its freight of beans. Fat acorns are shaken from the oaks. The leaves become a blaze of color in the woodland and fall and are a rustling mat of discarded fiber. The grass withers and the last insistent aster is victim of the frost. A season is ended. Yet I know that no season ends, for it is a part of the whole; Autumn becomes Winter as Winter, in due time, will become Spring. The ripened apple is a parcel of seeds, pregnant with more apple trees, more apples, more seeds. The discarded leaves become the woodland's humus, the untidy litter out of which will grow more trees, more leaves.

And every March I know the truth of Autumn, which is the quickened truth of Spring. Every March I know that, whatever life is, I am a participant; that, wherever is the nature of time, I can know this moment, this day, this particular fragment of eternity.

The perfect March day seldom endures, since weather systems move swiftly across the land in March. But even when it is followed by a chill wind and a sleety rain, as it so often is, it has brought the promise. I almost wrote "the dream," but man is the dreamer, not nature. The perfect March day brings the promise, and man brings the dream to build upon it. That is man's unique possession—the dream, the hope, and the belief. If I were a woodchuck lured from hibernation by such a day, I would emerge into the daylight possessed of hungers rather than dreams, hunger for food and for a mate. I doubt that I would have even an inkling of a dream of clover fields and a warm June sun. Instead, I would more likely have a wariness of fox and dog and man and a suspicion of the open field. My instincts would be directed to survival and procreation.

And that difference, while it may not be the reason my remote ancestors rose on their hind legs and began to enlarge their brains, certainly makes meaningful the difference itself. I can wonder, I can dream, I am not content with mere survival and procreation. I would participate in this urgency of new beginnings by knowing life and creating something more than others of my own kind. For this moment, at least, I am almost a whole man, not a fragmented one lost in the midst of his own confusions.

And, on that perfect March day, I am at last able to face the fundamental questions, accept answers which, though they may be intensely personal in origin, are to a degree universal in their truth.

Who am I? I am the latest, but probably not the last, in an unbelievably long and complex line of changing life forms. Much simpler forms of life, biologically speaking, have persisted far longer than my own kind has yet persisted, and there are ancient forms of life which, in terms of efficient and persistent existence, are far more successful than human life has yet proved itself to be. But I have no knowledge of any other form of life that can live as variously and think and feel and create as successfully as I can. I know no others that are possessed of the capacity to hope and believe and dream as my own kind is capable of doing.

Knowing this, I can accept countless new beginnings, and I can reject the endings that have no validity in time or in the unending flow of life itself. I can accept a flow of life that amounts, in my conception of time, to endlessness.

Where am I? I am in one small valley on one relatively insignificant mass of land on a watery, minor planet in the solar system. That planet is circling a sun that appears to be a lesser sun in the firmament, but which provides the light and warmth and sustenance making possible all the kinds of life I know. The solar system is one of many in a universe of which I am aware, for the most part, only on cloudless nights, a universe vastly larger than I can readily comprehend. This planet, this solar system as far as I can know it, are part of a pattern complex beyond my understanding, despite all the knowledge my own kind has amassed. But this planet is proof to me of such a pattern, such a system of order and meaning, though I must take much of that meaning on faith.

What time is it? I can discover no absolutes in time. Time is all relative, whether I speak of today or of a million years, of one hour or of forever. Time to me is comprehensible in terms of experience, as a lifetime and its relationship to this earth where that life originated.

I am here, on this earth, with the incredible variety of life forms, and whether I like it or not I am a part of that here and now. Knowing that makes this world a somewhat less lonely place.

At this moment it is March, the time of exciting potentials, of living tensions and fertile urgencies in the world around me. The other questions, and there is no end to them, cannot be answered today. Perhaps there is no answer to them; but that, the knowledge that there are questions, is sufficient to make me what I am, a man aware of March, of Spring, of beginnings.

12

SPRINGSONG

The peepers are out of hibernation and shrilling, one of the oldest Spring sounds on earth and, to my ears at least, the theme song of early April. Just how far back it reaches, no one can say within a thousand years, but we know the frogs were here to see the rise of this continent out of the shallow seas thousands of millennia ago. So for millions of years this clear, bell-like, almost musical, mating call has been echoing Spring's urgency and exhilaration, and what I hear from the bogland is the Springsong of life itself.

Spring, of course, is primitive and timeless, the recurring phenomenon of surgent life renewing itself. It answers the summons of no calendar, not even the calendar of the stars, for it is compounded of the basic stuff of life and the thousands of conditions that must be so finely balanced and maintained to revive and maintain life. Spring is the pulse that throbs through the earth and quickens the human heart for the simple reason that man is a live and sentient part of the whole earth community. He feels these things whether he sees them or not.

I saw the first signs of Spring in the shifting of the sun's shadow back in January, when the river was iced over, bank to bank, and snowdrifts lay deep in the woods on the mountain. Those signs were no more than a promise, but I could not doubt that promise, having seen it fulfilled every year of my life. I can be skeptical of human prophecies about elections, the stock market, or tomorrow's weather, but I know the sun and the seasons are not going to change their course or their pace. I was disconcerted briefly the last week in March when a small flock of migrant robins arrived here in the valley in the midst of a chill and sleety rain. I was sure they had misjudged the season this time and would be backtracking at least a hundred miles within twenty-four hours. Perhaps they had miscalculated somewhat, but not as much as I had, for by noon the next day the cold rain ended, the sun came out warm and hospitable, and those robins were strutting the home pasture and finding the food they no doubt expected as their due from life.

It is of such minor experiences that faith is compounded, and doubt of my own human infallibility. In some matters I must confess that I am less informed than a robin. I can rationalize this by saying that I know enough to build a roof over my head and come in under it when Spring seems to be uncomfortably slow in coming or is wet and cold on arrival. But that is really no more than adaptation to an environment that I cannot really master. I can wall out the wind, roof out the rain, build a fire to fend off the cold, but the wind blows, the rain falls, and the cold deepens or abates despite any orders I may issue.

And Spring comes on its own schedule, not mine. I adapt my life to it, knowing that it never comes all at once. Spring is a consequence of many things made evident by only a few degrees' difference in the average daily temperature from one week to the next, by a few more minutes of daylight and a slight change in the angle of the sunlight that falls on my small part of the earth. Thus precarious are the conditions of Spring. They depend on such essentially minor changes that we would scarcely be aware of them if nature didn't respond. Thus precarious are the conditions of life as we know it, though our senses are so dulled that we need a calendar and a clock to tell us what month it is and the time of day.

Yet that life has been here a long, long time. The Springsong of the peepers was heard before man was even a glint in evolution's roving eye. So Spring is a great deal more than the passing of a mathematical equinox or the greening of the hills. It is, in a remarkable way, an annual season of proof—proof that life does persist, despite ice ages, volcanic eruptions, earthquake convulsions, and despite the essentially lesser human uproars and trumpeted marchings to and fro.

Man is a strange, perverse creature, having a proper pride in his own accomplishments but woefully lacking in the capacity to admit his own ignorance and his own failures. As a race, that is; as a species. There are the chronic confessors, of course, just as there are the chronic braggarts. But the best man has been able to do with Spring is to chart it astronomically, then cooperate with it when it comes. Of all the ingenious machines man has ever devised, not one can create a living flower. We can incubate birds, artificially inseminate women and cattle, force bulbs, grow lettuce in a greenhouse; but in every instance we have to abide by rules that governed reproduction and growth for eons before man outgrew the tadpole stage and shed his gills and tail. And we still can't change the rules.

Down the road, my nearest neightbor is preparing to do his Spring plowing and planting. Albert has good, modern farm equipment, as good as money can buy. But when he starts his plowing—perhaps tomorrow if it doesn't rain again—he will merely stir the soil, break up its surface, aerate it, mix in the Winter manure from his cow barn, and add a few bags of chemical concentrates. Then, at a time dictated by wind and weather, he will plant oats and corn. And from that moment on he will depend on the soil, the sun, the rain, and the more or less varying conditions of nature. Beyond cultivation to discourage weeds, competitors of the corn he hopes to harvest, there isn't much he can do except hope that his degree of cooperation with those fields and the season has been sufficient and wisely planned and executed.

The farmer knows this. It is a truth that anyone close to the land grows up and lives with all his life. It becomes a part of him and inevitably shapes his way of thinking. Spring follows Winter, Summer follows Spring, and after Summer comes Fall, then another Winter, the round of the seasons, eternal change within the framework of eternal continuity. And life, the insistence of the seed, the root, the stem, the leaf, and the seed again. The two are irrevocably entwined.

I sometimes wonder if mankind doesn't get itself into periodic trouble largely because it herds itself so persistently away from such fundamental matters as Spring on a hillside. There, of all places, cause and effect are made manifest. There the celebration of such a simple, fundamental fact as life itself is too obvious to be ignored.

Every year holds one moment, which may last only a few hours or may continue for several days, when anyone with enough awareness to know high noon from midnight can see and sense such matters. It is that moment when the inevitabilities of

Spring are trembling on the verge of achievement, when tree and bush and vine are beginning to burst bud and achieve the miracle of the first green leaves.

Such a moment is here today. I saw it come, and, because I saw the day come with it, it was like being a witness at Genesis.

Because I dislike haste, confusion, and what we call the pressures of modern living, I begin my day early, when the day itself seems unhurried. So I was up before sunrise this morning, when the stars were just beginning to dim and the sky was filling with the glow that is less light than promise of light to come. I made coffee and turned out the lights and stood at the window with a steaming cup and watched the glow spread and the stars vanish. Then I went outdoors.

A robin was calling, a tentative call as though asking who else was awake. There was an answer from another robin. Half a dozen birds began to sing, rather quiet songs as though they, too, were still waking up. The grass underfoot was wet with dew and mist hung over the river. The maples on the river-bank were still shadows against the sky and the mountain beyond the pastures was like a deep, dark cloud on the horizon.

Then the stars were gone and the promise of light had become a glow in the east, a glow that strengthened and spread, minute by minute. The birds were louder now, and there were no soloists—they had become a chorus. Like dawn itself, they were unhurried. I have yet to see or hear a day begin with a rush. Daylight does not burst upon us, full of urgency; it comes almost catlike, stretching, opening its eyes slowly, looking at the world before it gets to its feet. It takes time even for the sun to rise.

I remembered the long-ago words of a wise old woman in

her nineties: "In the dawn of the day, when you seem to be the only person in the world, you know you have to make peace with yourself and with the universe." Then, with a smile, "Dawn is the nearest thing to youth that most of us know after we pass the age of twenty."

Now I know what she meant. Youth is innocence and wonder and belief. And no dawn I have ever witnessed was disillusioned or blasé or skeptical. All things are possible, at dawn, as in youth.

The first ray of sunlight touched the top of the mountain. I sensed it and turned and saw the dazzle of light on the distant trees, a brilliance that made the shadowed near slope of the mountain look pine-dark. It wasn't sunup here in the valley, but up there on the ridge was the golden light of a day that was coming, even down here beside the river.

The birds were silent, a strange silence, almost palpable, as though they were holding their breath. Even the breeze had quieted. The day was organizing itself, a day not one instant shorter or differently proportioned than Julius Caesar knew, or the Pharaohs, or the earliest cave man.

Then the sun was up. It lifted above the horizon and the long, golden light shone through the big maples, reached across the meadow, jeweling the wet, faintly green grass, leaping pools of shadow that still lay in every hollow. The sun came up in a vast silence, a great hush as of expectation. Then all the birds began to sing at once, like a great breath of exaltation, a chorus of affirmation.

There was a whole new day ahead, a day I had never known.

But the sense of wonder had still another dimension. The pear tree beside the garden was dressed in green lace, the leaves no larger than my little fingernail, the white blossoms still in bud. The dooryard lilacs were tufted at all their stem ends, each twin leaf cluster tipped with faint brownish purple as though the pinhead buds they clasped were oozing color, and not a leaf among them was big as a mouse's ear. The wild raspberries on the riverbank had scarlet tassels not half an inch long, each tassel an unfolding group of leaves whose shape and veining could be faintly seen. The early apple trees had gray nubs at their twig tips; when I drew down a branch to look closely I could see young leaf clusters just beginning to emerge from the buds, each leaf the size of a ladybird beetle's wing and each red-tipped as though blushing. The bridal wreath bush was green at every joint with tiny rosebuds of miniature leaves.

And there was that trembling moment. It is still here, three hours later, though changing moment by moment. It will be still further changed by this evening's dusk, and by tomorrow it will be still different. Life, like the dawn I witnessed, stands between promise and achievement. A new world, like the new day, is in the making in this old valley and on these old hills.

This afternoon I shall go for an exploratory walk across the pastures and up the mountainside, knowing I will find this same trembling moment there. On a certain ledge I will find hepatica in bloom, and in a well-hidden place there will be the sweet pink blossoms of trailing arbutus. A few wood anemones will nod on hair-thin stems beside an old stone wall where broad leaves and tense buds of orange-juiced bloodroot grow and wait. Early saxifrage will lift its eager tufts of tiny white bloom and lure early bees with yellow pollen. These things I know, knowing this moment, knowing that the wild-lings are celebrating life, in a sense, and preparing to beautify the earth. That is my human way of saying it, and I persist though I know that beauty is a by-product, not the purpose, of their existence. The mission of any leaf and blossom is to gather food, create seeds, and perpetuate the species. If the blossom or the leaf has beauty for the human eye, that is largely accidental, for the whole concept of beauty and esthetics is a product of the human mind. There were color and pattern, in the blossom even as in the sunrise or the rainbow, long before man's primitive ancestors were here to see them. They are still here, and if man is fortunate he finds pleasure in them.

When I see these things, as I saw this day begin, I am participating in life, and I ask no more than that of the world around me—the right of participation and the sense of wonder that accompanies it. I am, by the simple fact of being alive and sentient, a part of something magnificent and vastly more enduring than myself. I have an identity, though I am still only a minor member of the vast community of life. That membership is established, and I participate in something bigger than myself, more enduring than the human crowd. I am a participant in Spring, which by its very insistence gives the lie to all philosophies of chaos and futility.

It is the obviousness of Spring that both delights our hearts and baffles our emotions. Whether we willingly participate, Spring takes hold of us, shakes us, stirs our blood; for Spring is a quickening of the human pulse as well as a livening of the whole vital earth. We used to try to counter it with sulphur and molasses. We didn't trust it too far, and not without reason. Spring endangers maidenheads because Spring is no mere accident in the whole scheme of nature, which contrives first of all to maintain life and make sure of its renewal.

The sun I watched come up this morning rose just a trace north of east, and it will be in the sky today three minutes longer than it was yesterday, an hour and a half longer than it is out of sight on the other side of the earth. Astronomically speaking, that means Spring. In calendar terms, it means April. In the earthy terms of my own valley, it means slowly warming soil, frost oozing away, brooks full, and springs bubbling on the mountainside. It means that this is a somewhat more hospitable place to live than it was two months ago, not only for me but for every growing thing around me. It means me, going out to the vegetable garden with a fork to test the soil, and watching how the red, crinkly leaves of the rhubarb unfold, how the fine green shoots of the chives thrust up through the withered tangle of last year's growth; me, hoping there will be no late, hard frost to nip the daffodils already six inches high and in fattening bud.

Perhaps this is the wrong way to approach Spring, or to let Spring approach you. I have been told by those who follow other fashions than I do that life is a kind of disease and that we all live desperate lives in a chaotic world dominated by obsessive madness. In that sense, I suppose that Spring is only another example of senseless futility, since the leaf of April is doomed to October's sere discard and the whole begetting of the season leads to eventual death and decay. But somehow I cannot accept that philosophy. I know too much about growth and blossoming and seeding, the insistence and design of life. I have lived too long with the turn of the seasons to repudiate the present or doubt the future; and I know something of the past, having been a minor part of it myself.

Rather than in a world of madness and disorder, I find myself living in a part of a world of ultimate order and meaning where the only abiding confusions are those of my own kind. I have only to look around me to see that man is the incessant source of disorder and uncertainty. Perhaps that is a part of the price man pays for being a sentient creature with a memory, an imagination, and the capacity for worry and apprehension. Man is the only animal I know that is afraid of himself. I used to think that strangers to the open country made so much noise because they feared the silence and the human loneliness. Now I have my doubts. I suspect that they are afraid they may meet themselves coming around the mountain or through the woods. They know how dangerous they are and how little they can be trusted, especially when they are surprised or frightened.

The other morning I was out beside the old milk house I use for a garage, cleaning some of Winter's grime off my car, when an outland stranger drove up and asked directions. He was lost, and mine is not exactly a reassuring back road, but I was another human being and it seemed to bolster his confidence to hear my voice. He asked the usual outland questions; then, as defensive people so often do, he became personal. Wasn't it lonely away out here in the hills? Didn't I miss the culture and civilizing ways of the city? And, had I run away from people and their problems just to live a selfish hermit life?

I said no to all those questions, being patient up to a point. But when he demanded, in tones of accusation, why I didn't like people and wasn't interested in their problems, I knew I was dealing with a frightened man. He had stopped to ask directions because he didn't want to meet himself coming around the bend just up the road.

I said, "I still belong to the human race. I don't know of any way to resign, even if I wanted to, which I don't. I came up here to recall something about human dignity and to regain my perspective. It seemed important to get in touch again with realities. Maybe then," I said, "I could find some answers to the puzzle of this strange adventure, life."

"Have you found the answers?" he demanded.

"A few of them," I said. "More important, I found that the search itself is an important adventure."

He obviously didn't understand. He had lost his way again. So I gave him road directions and sent him back to the main highway.

But these are passing thoughts at this time of year, for man is really of slight consequence now, despite all his questioning. Man just happens to be here, one of those freaks of nature that appeared, like an *Amanita phalloides*, full of potent spores that proliferated in a favorable season. The earth tolerates him, with all his arrogance and predatory capacity; and someday the earth will fold over him again and grass will still grow, insects will still hum, wind will still blow, and water will run downhill, as they have since time began.

Meanwhile, we who know the touch of the earth wait each year for the season's mythical turn around the imaginary corner of the equinox. Then, by the calendar and the clock, come Spring and April. But we know that the clock of the seasons is in the earth, not in the stars. Spring is in a radish seed and an onion bulb and the root of a pokeweed plant. It is in the maple bud and a snapping turtle's deliberate pulse and a robin's gonads. How it got there, I do not know, as I don't know so many things that really matter. But there it is, ticking off the days and noting the angle of the sun and the temperature of the wind. I see the proof every year, and I am sure I shall see it recurring as long as I live. All those who come after me will see it, if they are still curious enough to look and interested enough to wonder. It is there now, ticking away, and I shoudn't be surprised if the peepers in the swamp down the road heard it the other evening when they began to yelp. To tell the truth, I would be amazed if they *hadn't* heard it.

So here I am, and there they are, and between us there is a large measure of understanding, whether others of my kind will admit it or not. I happen to call it April, and the peepers know it as mating time, the end of their long sleep; but we are talking about the same fundamental, which is life. Life that persists, in some form. Life that can be sweet. Life that surges in me, and in them, each time the cycle of the year reaches this point in its vast, mysterious, and endless rhythm.